Flint Architecture
of East Anglia

by

STEPHEN HART

BArch, ARIBA

with photographs by the author

dlm

First published in 2000
by Giles de la Mare Publishers Limited
53 Dartmouth Park Hill, London NW5 1JD
Reprinted 2002

Typeset by Tom Knott
Printed in Hong Kong
through Colorcraft Ltd

A CIP record of this book is available
from the British Library

ISBN 1–900357–18–6 paperback

Contents

Acknowledgements

I wish to express my thanks to J. P. S. Denny for showing me examples of decorative flintwork in North Norfolk, to Norman Scarfe, Andrew Harris and N. Hills for drawing my attention to particular flintwork techniques, to the Rev John Buchanan for his views on the east window of Barsham church, to Dr E. Robinson, A. England, E. Rose, J. J. Wymer, A. G. Parker and D. H. Kennett for much helpful information, to F. Avery for showing me how flint knapping is done, and to many other people who have given me help and advice in different ways. I also acknowledge my indebtedness to the authors of the works listed in the bibliography at the end of this book.

My thanks are also due to David Hudson and Wendy Newton, Mr and Mrs J. A. Joice, Mrs D. May, Mr and Mrs Hubert Sheringham, Mr and Mrs S. Warden, and Mr and Mrs Peter Warwick for their agreement to the inclusion of photographs of their houses in this book; and to the Norfolk Library and Information Service for permission to reproduce an illustration from Britton's *History and Antiquities of the See and Cathedral Church of Norwich*, 1815.

I also record my gratitude to the Marc Fitch Fund, to the Scarfe Charitable Trust and to the Norwich and Peterborough Building Society, without whose generous assistance this book could not have been published.

Foreword

I am honoured to have been asked to write a foreword to this important book. Having spent most of my life in East Anglia and owning a large number of flint buildings and walls, I am particularly interested in the subject. I feel sure that Mr Hart's book will become a textbook on the subject. The depth of his research and the extraordinary variety of the use of flintwork is truly remarkable and the book is made doubly enjoyable by the excellent photographs. May it have a wide circulation.

Grafton

EUSTON
THETFORD
NORFOLK

Introduction

Originating within chalk strata, flints occur in most of the chalkland regions of England. These lie mainly in a band to the south-east of the limestone belt and run from East Anglia to Dorset, taking in the Gog Magog and Chiltern Hills and the downlands of Hampshire and Wiltshire, with eastward branches encompassing the North Downs of Kent and the South Downs of coastal Sussex. Flints are also abundant in the coastal areas of East Anglia and in the glacial drift of later geological times which overlies much of the Home Counties north of London.

The regional character of the buildings in a particular locality derives to a great extent from their use of natural local materials, and as these are the legacy of the local geology, it is to be expected that buildings in different areas with a similar geology will have much in common. It follows, therefore, that flint buildings should be found in most areas where there is an abundance of this material and a deficiency in better building stones, and that their architectural characteristics are likely to be broadly similar. This is true for all of England's flint regions, except that certain techniques are only found in East Anglia. This makes East Anglia of special significance in the context of flint architecture generally because, whilst it can show virtually all the flintwork techniques that are used in the other flint areas, it is the only area where three important medieval architectural innovations occurred.

The first of these innovations was the building of circular church towers. There are about 170 of them in East Anglia and only six elsewhere in England (three in Sussex, two in Berkshire and one in Lincolnshire). Almost all of them are built of flint and they represent an early solution to the problem of building tall structures in an area where suitable stone for square corners was scarce. They established a continuing tradition that lasted from pre-Conquest times to the fourteenth century.

The next innovation, which first became evident in the late thirteenth century, was an architectural development of the round tower concept – the provision of an octagonal belfry on a circular ground stage. At first, this new shape for the upper stage was an integral part of a tower's construction from the outset; then later, while some towers were still built in this way, octagonal belfries were also added to many that had originally been wholly round.

The early fourteenth century saw perhaps the greatest innovation in East Anglia's flint architecture: a new art-form was born in which medieval masons exploited the contrasting qualities of knapped flint and limestone ashlar to create the unique regional style of architectural decoration known as flushwork, for which East Anglian churches are famed. The art persisted for almost two-and-a-half centuries until church building virtually ceased at the Reformation.

Flint Architecture of East Anglia is a tribute to the skills and invention of generations of East Anglian craftsmen who have given us an unsurpassed heritage of flint churches and secular buildings that are rich in a multitudinous variety of colours, textures and patterns.

It has not been possible to ensure that all the close-up photographs of the different types of flintwork are precisely to the same scale, but most of those taken at ground level were from a distance of about 1.2 m (4 ft), while those taken at a greater distance have been enlarged to compensate. Telephoto shots have been zoomed to give a comparable scale. The camera used was a Nikon FM with a 35 mm PC lens and a 100–300 mm zoom telephoto lens.

Throughout the book, black and white illustrations are referred to with roman numerals and colour illustrations with italic ones.

CHAPTER ONE

Origins and Nature of Flint

Over seventy million years ago, during the later stages of the Cretaceous geological period, huge chalk deposits were laid down in the seas which then covered much of the west European land-mass, including Britain. These deposits are widely spread over southern and eastern England and form the underlying strata of the western half of Norfolk and Suffolk, the north-west of Essex and south-east Cambridgeshire. In parts of Norfolk the chalk strata are more than 300 m (1000 ft) thick.

It is within the Upper Chalk, and in the top strata of the Middle Chalk immediately below, that flint in its natural state occurs. Here it is found embedded in the chalk rock in many forms, though most commonly as separate nodules up to 60 cm (2 ft) or more across. These may be of almost any shape but typically they are sinuous, amorphous lumps, often with knobbly protuberances and sometimes perforated. At some levels they lie in well-defined layers related to the bedding planes of the chalk, although generally their arrangement is quite random. Flint nodules in their original environment are visible in the faces of chalk quarries or in natural cliffs, as at Weybourne (1); and where the chalk outcrops on a beach, as at Sheringham (1), they can be seen at a stage in their age-long existence during which marine erosion is in the process of releasing them from the chalk.

Flint is composed almost entirely of silica and while it is extremely hard and durable, it is readily fractured by impact. Precisely how it developed in the chalk is uncertain, but it is chemically derived and its formation was probably a multi-stage process: a current theory suggests that it is a secondary replacement of the sedimentary fills of burrows within the host rock through the accretion and crystallization of dissolved silica deriving from the siliceous skeletons of sponges. Certainly the shapes of natural nodules and the manner in which they are embedded in the chalk lend credibility to the notion of their having formed within cavities.

Although all flint originated in the chalk, the processes of erosion have over millions of years freed nodules from this initial setting. Where chalk landscapes like those that bound

1   Flint nodules in course of erosion from a chalk outcrop on the beach at Sheringham

the western parts of Norfolk and Suffolk are not covered by glacial drift, loose flints in abundance lie scattered on or near the surface of the fields. Elsewhere, flints transposed by ancient sea incursions, rivers or land-ice meltwaters have been laid down as gravel beds, while others, engulfed by glaciers during the Ice Ages, have become constituents of the boulder clays, tills or clay-with-flints deposits that overlie the solid strata of much of East Anglia. During these transitions the appearance of the flints has often been changed by the conditions and forces to which they have been subjected since their release from the chalk. The field flints of the chalk landscapes may be broken unworn fragments still showing signs of their original contorted shapes, or they may be decayed or frost-damaged. Flints from the glacial tills are typically coarse and abraded, and water-worn flints from marine and river gravels or beach deposits (2) are mostly smooth and rounded.

Flints displaced by these geological processes have often become mixed with other materials which may have travelled considerable distances. Thus, accumulations of flint erratics, that is, those which have moved from their origins, may contain erratics of various rocks, many of which – like some of the flints – will have been worn into rounded cobbles and pebbles. It is not surprising, therefore, to find a few such non-flint erratics, or 'sarsens' as these alien stones are sometimes called, in rubble and cobble types of flintwork walling.

When first separated from the chalk, flint nodules have an opaque white outer crust known as the cortex, which is not, as might be supposed, an accretion of chalk but part of

2 Water-worn flint cobbles on Sheringham beach

the flint itself that has undergone a reduction in density and become porous. Where a nodule has been broken, the cortex often shows as a distinct white line, sometimes paper-thin, and sometimes thicker than orange peel, around the edge of the exposed dark core; usually the interface between core and cortex is very sharply defined.

In contrast to the crusty surface of the cortex, flint cores have a smooth texture with an almost vitreous lustre, and a fine flake chipped from a freshly fractured core will be seen to be translucent and a pale amber colour, while the core itself is usually dark – often almost jet black. Although black is perhaps the most usual core colour, there are variations in flints from different sources, and face colours of plain or mottled brown, olive, amber, grey and white are not uncommon.

The mutation known as cortication, which produces a flint's white cortex, appears to start at the surface and very slowly develops inwards, although the rate at which this happens is uncertain and seems to vary. When a flint has been split, the cortication process gradually begins to affect the newly exposed surface and in its initial stages may show as a transparent milky film over the core, producing shades of blue-black fading to blue-grey and then white as the incipient cortex imperceptibly thickens. The knapped flints of many medieval buildings display beautiful shades of blue-grey ranging from dark to light; but surprisingly, similar flints in other buildings of the same age have kept their pristine black-ness. The same phenomenon can also be seen on Victorian buildings that are only a quarter of the age of the medieval work, and so it is not really possible to deduce reliable indi-cations of the rate at which cortication occurs from the evidence of buildings.

A flint's surface may be changed by another phenomenon known as patination. Not to be confused with the whitening associated with the early stages of cortication, this affects some corticated flints but not others. Patinated flints are characterized by a waxy sheen suggestive of the nature of polished ivory, typically yellowish-white, but also stained to other shades; the patina is acquired through the assimilation by the surface pores of the cortex of new silica derived from soil water, a process that ceases naturally once a surface film has closed the pores. Patination is in a sense a reversal of cortication in that it repre-sents an increase in the flint's surface density, but apparently some degree of cortication is a prerequisite. It is a very slow process and implies great antiquity.

In all its forms, flint is liable to secondary coloration through the percolation of its pores by iron oxides or other pigments in solution; such coloration of the core is a much slower process than the staining of the cortex. Shades of brown, amber, yellow or grey are the more usual colours for flints found in fields or taken from gravel pits, while water-worn flint cobbles and pebbles that abound along stretches of the coast are predominantly grey, and they owe this, not to staining, but to incessant battering against each other in the waves along the shore. This will have completely or partly removed the cortex and dulled the black core to an even grey in the same way that fragments of glass, similarly bruised, become 'frosted'. Some unstained beach flints from which the cortex has not yet been worn away may be pure white, honed to an eggshell smoothness, and others, where the wearing has progressed further, may be partly grey with residual patches of the cortex colour.

CHAPTER TWO

Constructional Features of Flint Walls

'As-found' flint in all of its natural forms has been used for the construction of traditional flint walls, with similar material or a cut variation for the exterior face. The facing flints would probably have been laid first, with larger ones at intervals penetrating into the body of the wall to assist in bonding the face to the core, the core material then following. In addition to flints, the core material may sometimes include chalk, carstone or ferricrete in those areas where it was readily available. The thickness of a flint wall naturally varied in accordance with the size of the structure it supported, but the minimum normal thickness for cottage walls would have been about 45 cm (18 in), and even boundary walls were seldom much less. Some church tower walls are as much as 1.5 m (5 ft) thick.

Building flint walls demanded considerable skill. As with building brickwork, pieces of flint were individually set in mortar; but because of their irregularity in shape and size, generous quantities of mortar were needed to provide an adequate bed and fill the spaces around and between them. Initial lack of mortar adhesion to their smooth surfaces, the rounded shapes of much of the material and its unabsorbent nature meant that the mortar had to be of a stiff consistency to discourage the flints from settling or slipping out of position; and as the lime mortar used needed some time to attain its full strength, only a limited amount of wall, perhaps 30 cm (1 ft) or so at a time, could be built without intervals for the mortar to harden. Otherwise there was a risk of the work bulging or collapsing. Furthermore, in medieval times construction was discontinued during the winter because of the risk of damage by frost. Building progress was therefore slow, and the distinct changes in appearance that occur at about 3 m (10 ft) intervals in the walls of some round church towers, for instance at Bessingham (3), suggest that this measurement represents the annual rate of building these towers achieved at the time.

A characteristic constructional feature which can often be detected on many medieval flint buildings is the arrangement of 'putlog' holes. These are the holes formed in the wall during its constructon to accommodate the ends of the cross-members of the scaffolding

3 The round tower of Bessingham church, showing
changes of material within its height

that supported the walk-boards. They were afterwards generally filled with matching flint, leaving little, if any, trace; but their positions are often marked by a longer flat flint or a piece of stone over the filled hole. Occasionally even short, thin wooden planks can be found, as in the tower walls at Pentlow. From the fourteenth century onwards, the holes were sometimes lined with bricks – two header bricks on end, bridged by a stretcher (2). Irrespective of the type, their pattern within a wall surface can often be traced: they are usually about 2 m (6.5 ft) apart horizontally and approximately one above the other at vertical intervals of about 1.5 m (5 ft). On Little Waldingfield church tower they are particularly distinct as their filling material has been recessed.

COURSING

In addition to the intrinsic qualities of the material, the disposition of the individual pieces of flint in a wall has a pronounced effect on its appearance. Six arrangements as described below can be identified, although not all of these are applicable to every flintwork type, nor are they all receptive to galleting (see page 9 and glossary).

Uncoursed arrangements, which are compatible with all kinds of flintwork, are those where the materials are set in a random fashion without any alignment of their constituents (26, 31). To a greater or lesser extent – according to their spacing – the separate pieces engage with each other to give an overall texture free from any directional emphasis. This is a mode that is especially appropriate to material of non-uniform shapes and sizes; but a good appearance depends on a consistent and sustained balance of scale and texture over the whole wall area. Often, large expanses of wall are marred by changes in this balance, which can result in a patchy effect.

In *Coursed* flintwork (27, 95) the material is laid in definite horizontal rows and though there may be variations in the shapes and sizes of the pieces depending on the type of flint, there will almost inevitably have been some selection to achieve regularity in height. Except in the squared varieties of knapped flint, there is usually no attempt at 'bonding' successive courses by arranging the stones of one course so that they lie over the perpends (see glossary) of the previous one – in fact, because of the irregularity of the material, this is virtually impossible. What is of more importance for a good appearance is that the spacing between each piece should be fairly constant, and this factor determines the relationship of pieces in adjacent courses.

Rough-Coursed walling (30, 32) is a type where the material is built to rather imprecise levels, lacking the strong linear emphasis of coursed work. When viewed at a distance of more than about 3 m (10 ft), some examples give the initial impression of being uncoursed, and others of being coursed or partly so. It is usually those built with the rougher varieties of flint that create the former effect, but on closer examination their material will be seen to be set in more or less regular layers, even if with some deviations. It is the irregularity of the flints that gives the initial impression of randomness. On the other hand, in walls of more even material, sporadic horizontal alignments may be apparent although their continuity is often curtailed by the merging of courses or through the intrusion of occasional larger flints and other distortions.

An unusual coursing variant that is occasionally found can be called *Dual Coursing* since it comprises alternate courses of two different heights. The deeper courses may be some 15 cm (6 in) high and consist of large pieces of flint or erratics of irregular shapes, leaving much exposed mortar between them; the shallower courses are of similar irregular material but considerably smaller, on average rather less than half the height of the larger – with the result that in addition to the difference of course depth, there is a difference in the scale of the rhythm created by the pieces. To some extent the small pieces partially penetrate the gaps between the larger ones, and, in conjunction with intermittent crude galleting, tend to disguise the coursing, and so create an impression of random work. The

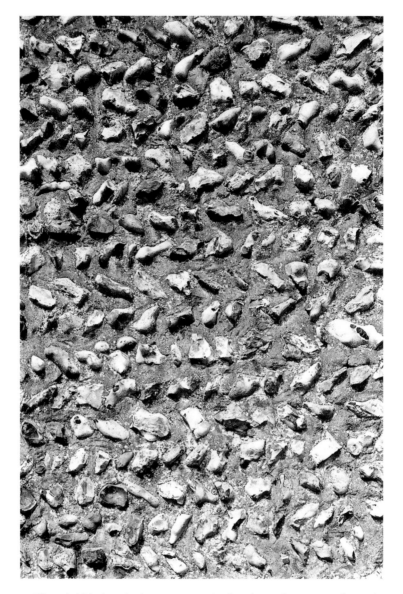

4 Flints laid in herringbone pattern in the eleventh-century chancel walls of Forncett St Peter church

example illustrated (3) appears in certain areas only of the walls of the majestic tower of Elmswell church.

Herringbone technique is not so much a method of coursing as a particular way of setting individual pieces. By its nature it can only be used in coursed work and it is characterized by the flints, usually of an elongated shape, being set at an angle, with their direction of slope alternating in consecutive courses. Rubble flint pitched in the herringbone manner is best seen in the eleventh-century north and south chancel walls of Forncett

St Peter church (4) where it is noticeable that even though the coursing and the alternating inclinations of the flints are quite distinct, the individual pieces themselves are irregular in shape and quality, some not even being elongated. All the same, the zig-zag rhythm is still sustained over appreciable areas. This type of work also occurs in other early church walls, for example at Shereford and Rockland All Saints in Norfolk, and Debenham in Suffolk, though it is not so well defined at these places as at Forncett St Peter. Eleventh-century instances of this practice are the equivalent in flintwork of the herringbone masonry seen in early stone churches in other parts of the country. Later, rather patchy, herringbone flint-work can be seen in the walls of Stalham church, but because of the extent of the Victorian restorations there, it is difficult to be certain whether this is nineteenth-century or medieval work. There is no such doubt, though, about the date of Bawdeswell church: built in the early 1950s, it has herringbone walls of flint pebbles incorporating a simple open-chequer pattern of buff brick headers (66). However, in general, herringbone patterns from medieval and later times are not common in East Anglia.

Also called 'stratification', *Layer Coursing* is a technique associated more with the flintwork of the late eleventh, twelfth and thirteenth centuries and is mainly found in walls of rubble flint. It shows as a series of distinct horizontal bands about 30 cm (1 ft) high which, in coursed flint, are defined by a slight thickening of the mortar joints between each band, and in uncoursed work by a levelling of the irregular flints to a straight line at the top of each band. The bands probably represent the extent of construction between the intervals that had to be allowed for the mortar to harden – it should be appreciated that the walls of circular church towers on which layer coursing is evident may be as much as 1.2 m (4 ft) thick or more. A striking instance of stratification shows on the thirteenth-century round tower of East Walton church (4) where forty-two quite distinct bands can be counted between ground level and the belfry cill level: they average a little under 30 cm (1 ft) in height and show up very clearly where the uncoursed flints are brought to horizontal levels at successive building stages. Examples in coursed flint can be seen on several early churches: the Norman round tower at Kilverstone and the thirteenth-century one at Pentlow have well-defined bands of five, four and three courses of flint, and other examples are certain walls at Castle Acre Priory, the east wall of Cockley Cley church and the remnant of a ruined wall at Flitcham church.

GALLETING

Galleting is the practice of inserting small pieces of stone, flint or other material into the mortar joints of a wall before the mortar has hardened and is mainly associated with walls of flint or inferior building stones whose uncertain shapes demand a generous measure of mortar surrounding each piece. Its original purpose was probably functional – as packing and wedging to the irregular walling material, or to give additional strength and weather resistance to the wide mortar joints – but in the course of time it became simply ornamental and developed into a distinctive local trait.

Galleting originated in medieval times, but it is difficult to be certain when it was first used, primarily because early medieval walls often contain fragments of flint of a size that makes it debatable whether they were built as part of the wall or inserted into the mortar, and secondly because many old flint walls are not seen today in their original condition, having been repointed at one or more stages of their life. However, it seems that galleting with flint flakes, an expedient use of the by-products of knapping, was contemporary with the emergence of knapped flint walling in the fourteenth century. Certainly, by the beginning of the fifteenth, the craft had reached a high degree of sophistication as is exemplified on Norwich Guildhall (1407 to 1413), where unshaped, knapped flints appear to have been deliberately set widely apart to allow the massing of a profusion of flakes around each individual flint, clearly with decorative rather than functional intent (5).

Though they rarely show the exuberance of those at Norwich Guildhall, flint flakes and fragments were the chief galleting material throughout the Middle Ages and later on, most usually in knapped work and in walls of mixed knapped and whole flints. Quite different effects were produced according to how the galleting was done. For instance, in some walls where the flints fit closely and the gallets are the same colour as the flint, they may be hardly noticeable; but where the flints are ill-fitting and have wide mortar joints, the galleting pattern may be the dominant feature of the wall.

As flint came into more general use, some walls of mixed materials and coarser types of flintwork also incorporated galleting, not only of flint flakes but also of little shingle pebbles (6), broken brick fragments (7) and, particularly in west Norfolk, chips of carstone (8) that have sometimes been mistaken for clinkers. All these types of galleting may also appear in Norfolk's chalk and carstone walls and even sometimes in brickwork. An example in a wall of mixed carstone and ferricrete is the late medieval tower of Wimbotsham church.

Although galleting of coursed cobble and pebble walls with flint flakes is a striking feature of some towns on the south coast of England, this practice is not an East Anglian tradition and is only rarely found in East Anglian cobble walls (14); neither does it ordinarily have a place in flushwork (Bunwell church porch is an exception), or in walls of squared knapped flint in which the material is laid with such precision that little if any mortar shows between the pieces.

QUOINS

Flint is an awkward material for constructing the angles of a building, and so walls built of it nearly always have stone or brick on the corners and at the door and window openings. Nevertheless, there are many instances where flint has been used in these positions too, both in pre-Norman buildings and those erected after the Conquest, when limestone became available and was generally preferred.

The naves of quite a number of early churches – Wramplingham, Pentlow, Thorpe Abbotts and Framingham Earl, to name a few – have flint quoins and on the latter they are

5 Flint quoins on the thirteenth-century tower of Beeston Regis
   church

formed with large lumps of flint cut to a right-angle, although this is hardly an improve-
ment aesthetically. Several eleventh- and twelfth-century church towers also have openings
with flint jambs and arches, as at Forncett St Peter and Great Dunham; likewise, in the
blind arcading which encircles the towers of Tasburgh (9) and Thorington, the jambs and
arched heads of the shallow recesses are all executed in rubble flint as used in the rest of the
tower wall. Flints form the corners of the Norman bell-stage of Guestwick church tower
above mixed limestone and ferricrete quoins in the lower Saxo-Norman stages; the tower
of Beeston Regis church, probably of the thirteenth century, has quoins of large uncut
flints for most of its height (5); and at Rackheath church, mainly of the fourteenth century,

6 Quoins of carstone and Barnack limestone on the nave of
St Andrew's church, Barton Bendish

there are rubble flint quoins on nave and aisle. The fourteenth-century octagonal tower of
Kettlestone church and the octagonal belfry on the round tower at Croxton have flint
angles, and fifteenth-century flint quoins are found on the widened nave at Warham St
Mary and on Heigham tower, Norwich, the only part of the church still standing after
wartime bombing. Large boulder flints are used on the corners of the late-seventeenth-
century Hastings Pew at Melton Constable church.

 These buildings provide convincing evidence that the tradition and skills of building corners in flint survived, if to a much lesser extent, for a long time after limestone had first become available in East Anglia in the eleventh century.

With some exceptions, quoins formed with ferricrete or large erratics are probably of a pre-Conquest date. Typically rather crudely shaped, and sometimes comprising quite large blocks, like flint quoins they have most frequently survived at the corners of the west wall of a church's nave, as at Bessingham (3); and where an aisle has been added at a later date, as at Wickmere, the original nave quoins have often been left undisturbed and show as a straight joint where the newer work abuts the old. Occasionally, carstone or ferricrete quoins are laid alternating with limestone as on the tower at Guestwick and the nave at Barton Bendish (6): these are probably Saxo-Norman, as the presence of dressed limestone implies a post-Conquest date.

Reclaimed Roman bricks are not uncommon in the flintwork fabric of early churches, and they have been used as quoins both alone and together with other material. The Norman church at High Easter has nave and chancel quoins (10) entirely made of Roman bricks about 4 to 5 cm (1.5 to 2 in) thick; a few Roman bricks are also laid in herringbone fashion in the walls, and at Great Melton thinner ones are intermixed with cut flints in the quoins, though these may be nineteenth-century restorations.

While some medieval flint buildings such as the church towers at Ashby and North Cove (11) have brick corners and dressings, the quoins in the majority of flint churches and monasteries built after the Conquest are of limestone. The stone came mainly from Barnack near Stamford and Caen in Normandy, from where it could conveniently be brought by water. Both these types of stone are freestones capable of receiving carving. 'Long-and-short' quoins, in which long stones laid vertically alternate with flat ones laid horizontally (7) are usually regarded as Saxon, but because of the scarcity of limestone in East Anglia in Saxon times, those on Great Dunham church and others elsewhere in East Anglia are perhaps more likely to be of a post-Conquest date. Stone quoins of the Norman period (8) were typically small, squarish and without much variation in size, and so the bonding between stone and flint was generally rather minimal; they also sometimes have a small roll-moulding worked on the angle like those at Ousden (8) and St Peter's, Duxford, or on the apse buttresses and nave at Hales.

Frugal unmoulded quoin stones with meagre bonding to the flintwork persisted well into post-Norman times; but progressively, bigger stones giving a better interlock with the flintwork came to be more widely used, as can be seen on many of the Wool Churches.

An interesting sixteenth-century quoin detail appears on the corners of the coursed cobble walls of Hempstead church porch (12). A flint cobble, knapped on two faces at right-angles, forms the corner of every other course, while the corners of the intervening courses are single Tudor bricks laid alternately as headers and stretchers. This is a rare detail and seems to be peculiar to the Sheringham area. A more recent interpretation of the detail is incorporated in the quoins, window and door openings and the chimneys of the 1934 restoration of a seventeenth-century sea-front building in Sheringham. Such departures from the established traditions, however, are not common.

Although, of course, there is variation from place to place, typical East Anglian bricks

7 Long-and-short quoins of Barnack stone on the eleventh-
century tower of Great Dunham church

are warm reds, except in those areas where lime-rich clays yield the so-called white bricks (in fact, usually grey or pale buff). The red varieties make a telling contrast with most types of flint, and, used as quoins and dressings, and indeed often at random among the wall flints, they undeniably enliven a wall's appearance. By comparison, the association of flint with the paler bricks can often give a rather drab result, except where the flintwork is substantially black. Sometimes brick quoins and dressings have been painted white, and while this is not a practice generally to be encouraged, with the right type of flint and in appropriate surroundings it can look very effective.

Brick corner quoins are sometimes formed with alternate headers and stretchers like

8 Norman stone quoins on Ousden church tower, the lower ones
plain and the upper ones with nook shaft

those of the window jambs of a house in Littlebury (*13*), or with steppings at each course (*14*). Usually though, they consist of small parcels of bricks laid in distinct blocks with one face longer than the other, and built one above the other with their long and short faces showing alternately on each elevation (*9*). Traditionally, corner quoins are three courses high, one-and-a-half bricks wide on the long face and one brick wide on the short face, though it is not uncommon to see them four, five or more courses high with wider long and short faces. But the difference in width between the two faces, which creates the bonding with the flint, is usually only half a brick.

Other deviations from these common patterns are to be found. For instance, the version

9　Orthodox brick quoin arrangement　　　　10　Partly staggered brick quoin arrangement

where alternate quoin blocks have two long faces and two short faces, and the intriguing type which, when viewed on each elevation separately, looks no different from the orthodox type, but when seen on the angle confounds immediate analysis: scrutiny of its coursing reveals that, instead of long and short faces coinciding on the two elevations, they are staggered relative to each other by one course (10).

Dressings to the jambs of doorways and windows are similar to those for corner quoins except that their face widths are usually less, often consisting of one brick and half a brick (24).

The form of all these brickwork quoins highlights the difference between the inherent structural natures of brickwork and flintwork, and can be readily appreciated as a logical architectural expression of the greater stability that brickwork imparts to the corners of a flint building. It comes as a surprise, therefore, occasionally to find a quoin arrangement that completely reverses this logical relationship of brick and flint. One such instance occurs in the village of Litcham where an otherwise orthodox brick-fronted Georgian building has 30 cm (1 ft) high quoins of natural flint nodules separated by single courses of brick: thus, paradoxically, flint assumes the task of expressing strength at the corners. Seen from a distance, however, the superficial resemblance of these quoins to rock-faced rustication of the kind associated with stately classical buildings suggests that they may have been conceived as an interpretation of that precedent in a local material, inspired perhaps by the Triumphal Arch of *c.*1730 at Holkham (*15*), designed by William Kent. On this building, as also on the same architect's Temple of 1746 in Euston Park near Thetford, rugged natural flint nodules, set well proud of a buff brick background, are used in the same manner to impressive effect, not only for quoins but for large arch voussoirs and wall rustication, too. Similar features also enhance the red-brick base storey of the look-out tower at Westwick; and quoins of this kind form the south corners of the stuccoed walls on the nearby Lodges that flank the main road.

A bizarre caricature of this type of flint rustication appears on a small nineteenth-century house at Cley next the Sea where panels of flint nodules, similar to those in the quoins at Litcham, are framed by the knuckle-ends of animal bones (*16*).

ARCHES

William Kent's noduled voussoir arches at Holkham and Euston are exceptional and are not therefore representative of the East Anglian flintwork tradition. It is from medieval churches that a simpler development appropriate to the material emerged: refined from fourteenth-century prototypes such as the fan-like array of bricks within the rubble flint above the west window of Market Weston church tower (*17*), this idiom comprised a pattern of single bricks set about 7.5 cm (3 in) apart, radiating from the focus of the arch with two or three squared knapped flints filling the spaces between (*18*). Often the bricks were in pairs, as over the windows of the church porch at Badwell Ash (*19*) and on the towers at Woodbridge, Ixworth and Elmswell, among others. A common variation on this theme is the use of small ashlared stones instead of bricks (*40*); and sometimes knapped flint alone creates the voussoir pattern, as in the arches of the aisle windows at Loddon. On Hemingstone church tower, ashlar stone and bricks are alternately interposed between the knapped voussoir flints (*20*); and on the church porch at Ashill and over the tower west window at Great Waldingfield (*11*) paired Roman bricks separate the arch flints.

Often seen above the hoodmould (see glossary) of stone doorways and windows, arches of these patterns appear on many East Anglian churches, Blakeney for instance having red bricks in the aisle window arches and limestone in those of the clerestory windows. There is a reflection of this concept on the porch doorway of Ixworth Thorpe church where, the wall material being brick, the customary relationship of flint and brick is reversed and it is the grey knapped flint between the red brick voussoirs that provides the contrast.

From these medieval brick-arch precedents, there evolved in the eighteenth century a development that was suited to the shallow segmental heads of domestic windows and doorways: in essence this was a half-brick arch with some whole brick voussoirs projecting upwards into the surrounding flintwork, thus giving the top line of the arch an indented

11 Arch formed with knapped flints and Roman tegulae in the fifteenth-century tower of Great Waldingfield church

profile. Several versions of this indented arch pattern are found, two of the most common being those where the headers and stretchers alternate radially (*13*) and the type where groups of two or three stretchers-on-end form a central 'keystone' with similar groups at the springer points (*24*). An early example of the latter is found on a cottage dated 1713 in Barton Bendish – in this case the arch bricks are pale gault and the walling is a mixture of flint, carstone, limestone and brick. These arch patterns, relying for their visual effect on the difference and contrast between the materials of arch and wall, can easily be understood to have evolved within the flintwork tradition, and they are characteristic features of Norfolk and Suffolk vernacular architecture of the eighteenth and nineteenth centuries. The detail is also found where brick arches are used in walls that are built of chalk or carstone.

CHAPTER THREE

Flint Building through the Ages

East Anglia is poorly endowed by nature with good building stone: the brown carstone found in west Norfolk is mostly harsh and rubbly; chalk is not very suitable for outside use because of its poor weathering qualities; and the ferricrete from localized deposits and the septaria and crag which occur near the coast in Essex and part of Suffolk are all stones of inferior quality. There is, however, an abundant harvest of flint and it is this unpromising material, mastered by generations of craftsmen, that above all others gives many of the region's buildings their distinctive character. Flint buildings are found throughout East Anglia, though more commonly in the western half and in coastal areas, and the majority of Norfolk and Suffolk churches, and many in Essex, Cambridgeshire and Hertfordshire, too, are built with flints.

Near the coast, most of the flint used for building came from the beaches, but inland it was obtained from the fields, from gravel deposits or direct from its parent chalk in quarries and flint mines. The most famous mines were in the Brandon area where, 4000 years ago in Neolithic times, the ancient pits near Weeting known as Grimes Graves yielded high-quality flints for implements and arrowheads. Much later, Brandon became an important centre of the flint-knapping industry, especially for the production of gun-flints in the seventeenth century and later. Knapped flints for building, that is those having a severed face exposing the core, were also produced and supplied to builders in several qualities, varying from top grade squared flints to irregular fragments.

Flint was extensively used by the Romans. Large quantities of rubble flint set in mortar formed the core of the massive walls of their coastal fortifications, as can be seen in the great walls of Burgh Castle (73) at the mouth of the Waveney, built towards the end of the third century A D. These walls, some 3 m (10 ft) thick at the base, were faced mainly with split unsquared flints in bands of four or five courses, separated by lacing courses of thin red tile-bricks (tegulae) that extend well into the wall thickness to assist in bonding the facing to the core. The fact that these walls have endured 1700 years of East Coast weather is testimony to the strength and durability of Roman mortar.

In contrast to Roman work, Saxon and Norman walls were built mainly of unsplit rubble flints. The earlier work is characterized by flints of all sizes randomly laid or roughly coursed, with wide mortar joints between the irregular pieces, and these walls often contained quite large lumps of flint, carstone, ferricrete or erratics, especially in their lower parts. In later eleventh-century work the flints may be of a more regular size as in the round tower walls at Colney church. Not easily distinguishable from this style of workmanship, as-found rubble flints of moderate size and compatible shapes are characteristic, too, of Norman walls, and, while also built randomly, are more typically laid in courses, as in the church towers at Fundenhall and Haddiscoe. Large cleft flints, although sometimes present, as in the upper walls of the round tower at Gayton Thorpe church, are less representative of this period. An important aspect of Norman work which distinguishes it from Saxon in East Anglia is the use of limestone ashlar for quoins and doorway and window dressings, features which in minor churches were more usually formed in flint or ferricrete before the Conquest.

Although flint churches may have been built during the tenth century and before, no standing flint structures in East Anglia later than the Roman period can be authenticated as earlier than the eleventh, when flint again had become an important building material. At about this time, and perhaps earlier, the first of the circular flint west towers of some of these early churches arose, establishing the characteristic East Anglian round-tower profile which was to be built for more than three-and-a-half centuries. Until quite recently, it was a popular belief that they were originally freestanding and erected by the Anglo-Saxons for defence against Danish raiders; subsequently, it was said, churches were added to them and their use converted to bell towers. This theory is now discredited with the realization that many are clearly later than their churches and that many are of a post-Conquest date. It seems, therefore, that the purpose of the round tower was no different from that of the square one and was to house bells.

It may never be known for certain whether the circular west tower was an Anglo-Saxon invention or whether, as thought by some, the idea was introduced from the Continent. What is important is that, irrespective of where the idea came from, it quickly became accepted and spread throughout the region, no doubt because the concept was recognized as an appropriate architectural form for its function and, in a region lacking indigenous freestone, it was one that could be built in local material without the need of stone for square corners. That said, however, it should be acknowledged that there are several church naves with square corners formed with flints or ferricrete, which on the evidence of how the tower joins the west wall of the nave, apparently predate their round towers. This shows that the capacity to construct square corners in local materials existed before the building of round towers.

Of the 175 or so round church towers in England, all but six are in East Anglia, and all of those except one or two in carstone or ferricrete are built of flint.

After the Conquest, with limestone for dressings now entering the region, more square flint towers were built, but the circular shape persisted concurrently with the square one well into the fourteenth century. Natural conservatism seems to have ensured its continuation after stone had become available, and the circular shape would undoubtedly have shown considerable advantages in cost and convenience over the square one, which required stone quoins.

In the vicinity of former Roman settlements, early medieval flint buildings often contain re-used Roman bricks or tegulae: they are generally a good bright red and vary in size with lengths and widths of as much as 35 by 28 cm (14 by 11 in) but are seldom more than 5 cm (2 in) thick (10); or they may be of the smaller tegular form, about 1.5 cm (0.6 in) thick (73). In the Norman parts of St Albans Cathedral, Roman bricks are used for quoins, arches and window dressings as well as being generously distributed within the wall flint-work, and the tegular type is much in evidence in the nave walls of Reedham church where some of them are laid in herringbone fashion. In smaller churches they generally occur as random incidents amongst rubble flintwork and occasionally in quoins, as at Caistor St Edmund or High Easter (10).

During the thirteenth and fourteenth centuries, flints were usually more closely packed (45) than formerly, and disposed at random amongst the natural flints of these and earlier walls there is often a proportion of split flints: these should perhaps be regarded as 'fractured' rather than 'knapped' as they probably arise, not from skilled knapping, but from the reduction of larger flints to amenable sizes, the breaking off of awkward projections or the inclusion of broken pieces. The visual impression created by these walls is therefore fortuitous rather than the result of conscious aesthetic intent. Knapped or cleft flints, as opposed to coarsely-fractured ones, first occur amongst as-found rubble flintwork towards the end of the thirteenth century; and at about the same time, walls faced entirely with cleft or knapped flint (29) also began to appear, suggesting that split flints now came to be regarded as a means of creating walls of greater refinement. After that, during the fourteenth century, walls faced with irregular knapped flints, sometimes roughly squared (39), are not uncommon and the north wall of the Bridewell in Norwich, built in about 1370, is a fine example of fully squared knapped flint.

An important development of the late thirteenth and early fourteenth centuries was the incorporation within flint walls of a few locally made bricks. After the departure of the Romans, brickmaking in England ceased for about 900 years, and it was not revived in East Anglia, it is now generally believed, until the thirteenth century. Thereafter, medieval bricks appear here and there at random or in irregular patterns amongst the flints in some church and tower walls and especially in the framing and bridging of putlog holes; they were also used as external dressings to tower windows, and frequently for their embrasures internally, and also as quoins of octagonal belfries as at Wramplingham and Ashby, Suffolk. These early bricks are irregular in shape and vary in size but typically are about 24 cm (9.5 in) long by 11 cm (4.5 in) wide and generally about 5 cm (2 in) thick, although sometimes thicker. There was no standard size. Their colours are inconsistent and can vary from light yellow to plum red (11). Medieval bricks can be a useful aid in dating the structures in which they occur, and seem to indicate that many round church towers are not as old as has previously been thought.

The late thirteenth century also saw a prophetic architectural development of the round tower concept – the union of a circular lower stage with an octagonal belfry stage. Although it is widely supposed that all octagonal belfries on round towers were additions to Saxon or Norman structures, some towers have a wealth of evidence for the belief that their two stages may be contemporary and that the circular stage is post-Norman. This evidence includes the similarity of the flintwork in both stages, the absence of fabric variation internally at the level of the external change of shape, the use of medieval bricks in the fabric of both stages, the pointed tower arch, and the lack of any indications of former belfry openings in the circular stage, or of any Saxon or Norman evidence. Also, the low position of the first row of putlog holes in the octagons of some towers implies continuity of construction with the circular stage rather than addition to it.

Inspired perhaps by the fully octagonal thirteenth-century towers at Toft Monks and Buckenham, the earliest towers with an octagonal upper stage built from the outset on a circular base, for example those at West Somerton and Hassingham, have single lancet belfry openings with stone dressings and dressed stone angles to the octagon. At Ashby, probably a little later, the dressings of the lancets and angles of the octagon are formed in medieval brick. These towers were followed later in the fourteenth century by others with two-light belfry openings such as Ilketshall St Andrew, Thorpe Abbotts and several more. After that, in the fifteenth century, many of the older wholly round towers were given new octagonal belfries, which either replaced earlier belfry structures or increased the height of the tower.

On some, but by no means all, of the towers that were built from the outset with a round lower stage and an octagonal belfry, the external change of shape of the flint walling at the junction of the stages is achieved by a simple cambered merging of circle to octagon, without any form of string course. The fourteenth-century towers at Ilketshall St Andrew, Rushall and Wramplingham have this type of transition between stages, which, because it does not seem to have been used when manifestly later octagons were added to existing circular towers, could reasonably be considered as an indication of the contemporary construction of the two stages. When a later octagonal belfry in a different style was built onto an early circular tower, an intervening string course at the junction of the new to the old would probably have been regarded as essential, both aesthetically and constructionally, and this practice became the norm in those circumstances.

Fifteenth-century flintwork, both unfractured and knapped, is generally more carefully selected, graded and coursed, and walls were often faced entirely with knapped flints as several fifteenth-century Norwich churches show. Many walls of this period consist mainly of knapped flints with cobbles or unfractured flints and non-flint erratics (47), and this combination can almost be regarded as a standard mix of the fifteenth century. Such walls were often profusely galleted with flint flakes and fragments.

The mellow shades and textures of limestone make the perfect foil to the sparkle and lustre of knapped flint, and the contrast between these two materials is exploited to great effect in that splendid manifestation of East Anglian craftsmanship known as flushwork. This is a system of wall-surface enrichment in which ashlar limestone and knapped flint, both set flush with the wall face, were used together to create decorative architectural patterns. It originated early in the fourteenth century, and afterwards for nearly two-and-a-half centuries flushwork decoration on churches became widespread in Norfolk and Suffolk and to a lesser extent in Essex. The second half of the fifteenth and the first quarter of the sixteenth centuries were the golden years, and the finest work dates from this period. It was a time of prosperity arising from the wool and cloth trades, wealthy merchants giving or bequeathing large sums for new church building, rebuilding, extensions and restorations. It is the clerestories, towers and porches of these Wool Churches that exhibit the most spectacular flushwork, and there are many sumptuous examples throughout East Anglia.

Another type of wall ornamentation contemporary with flushwork, though considerably less common, is the technique known as proudwork (47). It also combines freestone and knapped flint, but unlike flushwork, the stonework projects from the knapped flint background and is usually moulded.

Limestone was also used to some extent in flint walls in a less stylish fashion: irregular small pieces were often freely interspersed amongst the flints and erratics of the fabric, particularly in fifteenth-century church walls (91). The practice of including occasional bricks continued, but not universally, and local stones, and sometimes other non-indigenous ones, were also incorporated in the flintwork in a similar way with the result that different mixes of flint, stone and brick produced walls of amazing variety and colour.

During the sixteenth century, the depletion of Britain's indigenous forests led to a decline in timber-frame construction for domestic buildings, and brick increasingly became the preferred material for great houses and manors. Flint was still used, although it no longer displayed its recent luxuriant craftsmanship, and indeed, on the walls and circular towers of Stiffkey Hall of c.1578 the flintwork was covered with rendering.

Split untrimmed flint, coursed and galleted with flint flakes, occurs on the outer gatehouse of Baconsthorpe Castle (1560); several smaller houses of the late sixteenth and early seventeenth centuries in north Norfolk, e.g. Edingthorpe Hall and Green Farmhouse at Thorpe Market, also have this kind of walling, while at Metton Manor Farm and Vale House, Stody, whole flints are interspersed among the knapped ones. The period also produced walls with a bolder texture in which coursed cobbles were set with about half their girth projecting from the mortar, as exemplified in many fine Norfolk barns like the one at Castle Acre, and in farmhouses of the time (83).

Flint came at this stage to be widely used for smaller houses, cottages, farm buildings and boundary walls. The customary thickness of bricks had by now increased to about 6.5 cm (2.5 in), and they were often incorporated at random or in patterns within the flintwork, and were almost universally used for quoins, dressings and chimneys, and sometimes for gable parapets or decorative corbelling along the eaves. And so, throughout flint terrain, this combination of materials and constructional details established a distinctive vernacular architecture that was to continue with little change into the early twentieth century. Within this tradition, walls show a wide diversity of appearance but all of them essentially rely on unsophisticated skills and the material at hand – flint as found or roughly split, and local brick.

12 Victorian chequer flushwork on the
south aisle of Elmswell church

In the eighteenth century, perhaps because it had become the common material for the
humblest of buildings, flint suffered a decline in its social status in favour of brick, which
was now considered a more fitting material for buildings of any pretension. This tendency
is evident from the number of houses of the period that have front walls of brick but use
flint for their side and rear walls, and for their outbuildings.

Stimulated by an impetus for church restoration, by some new church building and by
the development of coastal towns as holiday resorts, the interest in flint building saw a
revival in the nineteenth century. Many Victorian church restorations, regardless of their
architectural merit, exhibit coursed and uncoursed knapped flint of high quality (31): the
excellence of the flushwork on the south and east of the chancel of St Michael's at Coslany,
Norwich, carried out in 1883, and that on the chancel of Cromer church (35), built in the
same decade, show that the skills of this craft had not been lost.

Innovations and refinements to some traditional techniques also made distinctive con-
tributions to the flintwork idiom. One of these trends which blossomed in coastal towns
was the use of small beach pebbles not much larger than an egg, set so closely that the
mortar was virtually invisible. The immaculate virtuosity of walls faced in this manner is
an architectural delight, scarcely better exemplified than in the little school of 1830 at

13 Uncoursed pebble facing on precast
    concrete cladding panels on a modern
    block of flats in Sheringham

Overstrand (*28*) where the visual effect can be seen to depend on the careful selection of the pebbles for uniformity of shade as well as for size.

Victorian churches may show other types of interesting innovative flintwork as well, some of which are described later; but not all Victorian experiments were aesthetically successful. At Elmswell church (*12*), for example, a large and rigorously geometric pattern of knapped flint and stone has been applied on the east end of the south aisle where it is not only out of scale and quite unsuited to the shape of the wall it occupies, but is stylistically inappropriate on the walls of a Gothic church.

Towards the end of the nineteenth century and in the early twentieth, traditional vernacular practices were being superseded by more universal building methods and, particularly in the developing coastal resorts, by the fashions of the time. Flint came to be used more for its decorative qualities than for functional or economic reasons, and quite sophisticated knapped flint treatments were now not unusual on small villas in seaside towns (*33*).

Flint was little used in the twentieth century during the period after the first world war. But towards the end of the 1960s, an increasing awareness of the lack of local character in much new building and a wider appreciation of conservation issues became the catalyst for a gradual renaissance in flintwork. New methods of using the material for building were developed that were designed to overcome the scarcity of craftsmen skilled in laying flint. The essential departure from traditional practice in these new methods was in the concept

14 Precast concrete blocks faced with selected cobbles on system-built houses
    in Ladbrooke Place, Norwich

of precasting: concrete building blocks and panels, faced with various types of flint, were
cast in moulds under controlled factory conditions, which, when cured, could be fixed or
laid on site by relatively unskilled labour at a greater speed than by conventional methods.

Storey-height precast concrete panels surfaced with cobbles face the walls of a modern
church hall in the churchyard of Gorleston parish church, and comparable panels with
a knapped-flint finish are used as cladding on several modern buildings in Thetford.
On a modern block of flats in Sheringham (13) precast concrete cladding panels on the
window bays have a facing of uncoursed pebbles. Smaller precast building blocks faced
with neatly-coursed cobbles make a suitable cladding to system-built houses in Ladbrooke
Place, Norwich (14), and similar blocks faced with knapped flint clothe the structure of
Yarmouth House, a multi-storey office building in Great Yarmouth.

Recently, the old skills of laying cobbles in situ have been revived and adapted to modern
cavity-wall construction, and this kind of wall is increasingly to be found on new buildings
in flint areas. A confident modern example is the hall extension to St Mary's church at
Luton, and a pleasing group of small dwellings near the church at Upper Sheringham
makes an appropriate extension to the vernacular tradition.

CHAPTER FOUR

Local Flintwork Character

It is possible to associate certain kinds of flintwork with particular areas, although this does not necessarily mean that they are exclusive to those areas. Colour bias, idiomatic technique and untypical forms of the material make subtle variations from the commonplace and can give a pervading ambience to a locality.

The colours of much inland flint are due to pigments assimilated from the soil or gravel beds from which the material was obtained, the degree of staining being dependent upon the minerals present. Iron compounds are the most potent of the staining agents, causing shades of brown, orange, amber and yellow. These colours, together with grey, white and black, produce the typical colour blends of flint buildings and walls throughout East Anglia. But variations in the effects of the ground minerals can result in marked differences in the colour balance of as-found flint from place to place, to the extent that certain combinations with a distinctive chromatic bias are recognizable as being characteristic of particular districts.

Much of the flint in the Brandon area comes straight from the chalk and is unstained; knapped work is a pure strong black, and rubble and fragmented material are unadulterated black and white, while in neighbouring parts of north-west Suffolk and east Cambridgeshire cool grey-amber mixes are typical. Flintwork characteristic of south Cambridgeshire, west Suffolk and north-west Essex contains a greater proportion of broken flints and non-flints, so giving predominant tones of grey, black and cold brown that tend to create a rather sombre effect, particularly when it is associated with the local gault bricks. To the west of Cambridge, where non-flint cobbles almost eclipse the flints (89), the resulting emphasis is brown. In much of the rest of Suffolk, knapped flints and erratics are a common mixture found in many medieval churches (90), and in the coastal parts of the county where the core colours of the indigenous flints are shades of amber rather than the more usual black, the prevailing colours may be brown, amber, yellow and white, with no grey or black (24). In Norfolk, areas around Fakenham and East Dereham are characterized by fiery combinations of brown, orange and yellow flints with little, if any, black (25), generally in association with red brick; and a group of villages to the east of Downham Market where the local bricks are a lighter pinkish orange, display sunny mixtures of orange and yellow (8). Knapped flint of unusual whiteness is a feature of several churches in part of north-east Norfolk which can be seen in the porch and clerestory at Wickmere (40), the porch at Bessingham and the tower parapet flushwork at Plumstead. Grey littoral water-worn flints are much in evidence as cobbles and pebbles in places near the coast where they are often carefully selected and neatly coursed.

As well as colour variations, particular kinds of flintwork that are not universally found throughout the region may be associated with certain areas. Around Brandon, for centuries the centre of the flint-knapping industry, not only is there fine knapped work in many quite modest buildings, but, as might be expected, walling of knapped fragments – the waste from the knapping process – and near the Suffolk coast, walls faced with small natural fragments (24), as distinct from knapped fragments, make their own special contribution to the local vernacular. In Norfolk, at places between Castle Acre and the coast at Thornham, some unusually large flints are quite common and appear in buildings as rectangular knapped blocks (37); and in certain villages in the west of the county like Wereham, Stoke Ferry and Northwold one can see a local practice in which sized rubble in regular courses is galleted with neatly spaced carstone chips that form vertical and horizontal dotted lines in the bed and perpend joints (8). Domestic and farm buildings and boundary walls galleted with carstone, and to a lesser extent with pebbles or chips of brick, are more characteristic of west Norfolk than elsewhere; and where the carstone outcrops below the western edge of the chalk between Hunstanton and West Dereham, mixed flint with brick and carstone rubble is a common local combination (99).

Certain untypical flintwork techniques on medieval churches may also be found to be associated with particular localities. A case in point is the similarity of the tower parapets of several city churches in Norwich which have flush and low-relief decoration inset within knapped flint in an unusual style (27) that is only occasionally seen elsewhere; another is the stylistic kinship of the tower parapets built in proudwork, in itself a significant departure from the more universal flushwork, on three nearby churches at Mattishall (125), North Tuddenham and Shipdham. Near the Suffolk-Essex border the quite rare practice of coursing flint cobbles with Roman tegulae appears in some of the walls of a few churches, for example at Great and Little Waldingfield (75), Cavendish and Ridgewell.

CHAPTER FIVE

The Varieties of Flintwork

Since its earliest use, flint has been exploited in buildings in many different ways and combinations, making walls of great variety. It is a variety that derives nevertheless from the relationship of just two fundamentals: the materials and how they are laid.

Flint on its own appears in walls in several forms, as natural nodules, bruised boulders, fractured fragments, smooth cobbles and pebbles, and split or knapped pieces and as mixtures of these. Differences in the sizes, shapes and colouring of the separate constituents, the degree of their selection for particular characteristics and the proportion or dominance of particular forms in a mixture add further nuances. Any of such variations may also be combined with brick, limestone, carstone, chalk, septaria or erratics of sundry other rocks.

The methods of laying the flint are nearly as varied as the material itself. Different modes of coursing, close or wide spacing of the pieces and the galleting of mortar joints all contribute to this diversity. When other materials are combined with the flint, their incorporation can be effected in almost limitless ways, from the wholly random to the methodically patterned.

From this it will be evident that the flintwork spectrum is quite extensive. But in the existing literature of building, apart from generalized descriptions, there is neither a universal terminology for nor indeed any recognition of many of the techniques. So, in order to meet this deficiency and to differentiate between the numerous varieties of flintwork, the system of nomenclature and classification described below, and shown in the accompanying table, has been devised and adopted for this book.

Nine principal categories have been designated that are based on unmistakable visual attributes. Of these, three categories cover flint used by itself, comprising *As-Found* material, that is flint in any of its natural forms, *Knapped Flint*, that is material with severed faces, and *Compound Flintwork*, being mixtures of the two; four categories, in which flint types are not differentiated since this would result in almost limitless permutations, cover flint with other materials and include *Flint with Brick*, *Flint with Stone*, *Triple Composite*, that is flint with two other materials, and *Multiple Composite*, in which three or more materials are present with the flint; and two categories cover *Freestone Flushwork* and *Flushwork Derivatives* separately from flint with other materials, because they represent a specialist usage of flint that is exclusive to East Anglia.

Within these nine categories, specific types of flintwork are defined according to their characteristics or to how they are associated with other materials. Further distinctions within some of the designations could be made by reference to their styles of coursing and galleting, but these are not shown in the table for the sake of simplicity.

The flintwork varieties shown in the table and described in the ensuing pages are on the whole unambiguously recognizable from specific features, but not all flint walls will be found to conform exactly to particular classifications, some of them perhaps falling half-way between two types and qualifying to be classed as either of the two with equal justification. For instance, should a wall built of cobble flints and cobble erratics be classed as 'Cobbles' or as 'Flint and Stone Erratics'? Likewise, extraneous components such as occasional erratics or an odd piece of brick or stone may intrude into an otherwise well-defined type, and although they may not significantly change a wall's appearance if they are widely distributed, what proportion of them can be accommodated before uniform material becomes a mixture? These are matters for individual judgement and serve to illustrate that classification of flintwork is not an exact science but rather an aid towards a fuller understanding and appreciation of flint architecture.

FLINTWORK CLASSIFICATION TABLE

category	*type*
AS-FOUND FLINTWORK	Flint Rubble
	Flint Nodules
	Natural Fragments
	Cobbles
	Pebbles
KNAPPED FLINT	Cleft Rubble
	Knapped Fragments
	Knapped Select
	Knapped Ovals
	Knapped Scales
	Knapped Blocks
	Rough-Squared
	Squared
	Flakes
COMPOUND FLINTWORK	Mixed Flint
	Decorative Combinations

FLINT WITH BRICK	Random
	Chequer
	Flemish Chequer
	Open Chequer
	Morse
	Diaper
	Banding
	Free Motifs
	Framing
FLINT WITH STONE	Flint and Chalk
	Flint and Red Rock
	Flint and Carstone
	Flint and Ferricrete
	Flint and Septaria
	Flint and Crag
	Flint and Stone Erratics
	Flint and Non-indigenous Stone
	Flint and Stone Banding
TRIPLE COMPOSITE FLINTWORK	Flint, Limestone and Erratics
	Flint, Limestone and Brick
	Flint, Brick and Erratics
	Flint, Brick and Chalk
	Flint, Brick and Carstone
	Flint, Carstone and Chalk
	Flint, Carstone and Red Rock
MULTIPLE COMPOSITE FLINTWORK	Flint, Brick, Limestone and Erratics
	Flint, Brick, Ferricrete and Erratics
	Flint, Brick, Limestone and Carstone or Ferricrete, with or without Erratics
	Flint, Ferricrete, Septaria and Crag
	Flint, Brick, Ferricrete, Crag, Limestone, Septaria and Erratics
FREESTONE FLUSHWORK	Inset
	Chequer
	Emblems
	Tracery and Panelling
	Serial Flushwork
FLUSHWORK DERIVATIVES	Brick Flushwork
	Proudwork
	Relief Flushwork

CHAPTER SIX

As-Found Flintwork

FLINT RUBBLE

'Flint rubble' is a description that is applicable to flintwork containing different forms of as-found material: essentially it is non-uniform. Most commonly the components of flint rubble are field flints which may be of any size up to 30 cm (1 ft) or more across, and may comprise whole or broken nodules, angular fragments, worn or unworn cobbles and pebbles, degraded or pitted boulders, and occasional non-flint erratics. All these varieties of material may be laid coursed or uncoursed; but when they are laid coursed, there will inevitably be some selection for size.

As might be guessed, the appearance of rubble walls will vary subtly or obviously from one example to another in accordance with the forms, sizes and colours of the material, the proportions of each in a mixture, the spacing of the pieces (i.e. the amount of mortar showing), the extent to which the joints are flushed or recessed and whether the work is coursed or galleted. Surprisingly, galleting in rubble flintwork is not as common as might be expected, and, where flint gallets are used, they are often so irregular in size and distribution as to make them confusingly indistinguishable from the smaller walling flints.

Uncoursed, rough-coursed and coursed rubble flint walls of all kinds of as-found material have been built for a millennium, and a few examples illustrate the striking differences they can show. Flints laid randomly in masses of mortar may be early, or they may originally have been plastered and not been intended as facework, although now exposed where the surface rendering has weathered off: many such walls can be seen where remnants of plaster are still in place. Ungalleted rubble, selected for compatibility of size (*18*), creates quite a different effect, particularly where, due to centuries of weathering of the mortar, or careful repointing, the flints have a bolder projection from the face of the mortar. Cobbly rubble (*21*), where the flints are closely spaced with some uniformity of size and little mortar being visible, may give the initial impression that it forms a cobble wall, but closer examination will show that, while there are a few cobbles, most of the ingredients are rubbly material comprising mainly rocky-textured and worn boulders that are typical of glacial field flints.

Most rubble mixes contain a few cobbles, rough-cut pieces, non-flint erratics and one or two alien stones but in insufficient numbers to subvert the overall rubble bias; mixtures in which these feature to a significant extent would fall within other classifications.

FLINT NODULES

Typically, flint nodules have amorphous curvaceous shapes of almost sculptural quality and represent the material in its most elemental form, being largely unaffected by later processes of natural attrition or by the hand of man. They will probably have come directly from chalk pits or from the land surface in chalk areas, and they are prevalent where the flint-bearing chalk is not far below the surface; chalk-pits yield relatively larger nodules with a clean white cortex unstained by ground pigments. Nodules from the fields may be stained to shades of yellow and brown like some of those in the late-thirteenth-century chancel walls of West Harling church (22), where some broken and some roughly split nodules have been included.

Nodule sizes vary considerably, and because of this and of their contorted profiles, they are usually laid uncoursed or roughly coursed; but with skilful selection and placing they can be closely fitted without showing excessive mortar. This type of flintwork is not specific to any particular architectural period and examples from early medieval times onwards can be found.

A specialized use of natural flint nodules has been adopted in the walls of the East Lodges of Raynham Hall, dated 1925 (23). The flints used are of fairly uniform size and each has been carefully selected for the perfection of its cortex and the almost complete absence of black broken faces. Skilfully laid with the mortar hardly showing, the result is a richly textured surface of dazzling whiteness, set off by buff brick dressings.

Meticulous selection of nodules and mastery in their laying is also evident in William Kent's flintwork at Holkham and Euston that has been referred to. In the Triumphal Arch at Holkham, this expertise extends even to the use, in the lesser rustications of the smaller-scale side arches, of smaller flints than those used in the main arch rustications.

NATURAL FRAGMENTS

Essentially a form of flint rubble, this material consists of small fragments of naturally broken flint, irregular and angular in shape and fairly uniform in size, on average not more than about 7 cm (2.5 in) across. As broken fragments, most of the pieces expose surfaces of the core material, some of which are stained to shades of amber, and some corticated, and some display the age-old wax-like sheen of patination. In contrast to the sharp edges of flints broken or split by man, the arrises of these small fragments are slightly blunted, providing further evidence of their great age.

In a wall, the pieces are set uncoursed with bold projection from the backing and no mortar being visible. Their angular shapes allow very close interlocking and create a vigorous small-scale texture, with irregular facets of white adding reflective sparkle to tones of brown and amber – without grey or black.

There will have been selection of these flints for uniformity of size, and the practicalities of construction suggest that they will have been set into a surface rendering rather than being built up with the wall. Their rough profiles would provide an excellent key to the rendering.

This technique flourished during the nineteenth century in the coastal area of Suffolk between Aldeburgh and Southwold where it can be seen at several places, for example Blythburgh, Bramfield (24), Theberton and Westleton. In these parts it is usually found in harmonious association with buff brick dressings.

COBBLES AND PEBBLES

Cobble and pebble flints are flints which have been worn by water or ice into more or less rounded shapes with no sharp edges or corners, their contoured forms being suggestive of potatoes, buns, kidneys, pears and eggs. Some of them may be pitted or show weathered patches of the core where a fracture has occurred, and others, having lain undisturbed for aeons since attrition, may have become patinated. Specimens from the boulder clay, disfigured by glacial abrasion, usually have cruder shapes and rougher surfaces than water-worn ones from beaches or river deposits.

There is no intrinsic difference between cobbles and pebbles (the terms also apply to non-flint erratics of similar sizes and shapes) since the distinction between them is purely one of size, cobbles being the larger. A diameter of about 7.5 cm (3 in) is the generally recognized order of magnitude distinguishing a cobble, but as stones of ovoid shapes have more than one diameter, this must be a fairly flexible distinction. In practice – certainly in secular buildings – the size of the flints can often be gauged by comparison to the coursing of brick dressings: if three or fewer flints equate with three courses of brick (a common height for quoins), they can be regarded as cobbles; and if four or more equate with the same measure, then they are pebbles. An exception to this guideline occurs where small flints, clearly less than 7.5 cm across, are coursed to align with quoin bricks, leaving excessive mortar exposed. To summarize, pebbles are roughly egg-sized, while cobbles can be the size of oranges or coconuts and any size between. The larger sizes may be called boulders.

Coursed and uncoursed cobbles represent a significant aspect of East Anglia's vernacular architecture, being chiefly associated with houses, cottages, farm buildings and boundary walls, although they are also found on some churches, particularly near the coast.

Cobbles are traditionally set with generous projection from the mortar (25, 26) often with nearly half their girth showing: this gives such walls a lively texture with a strong play of light and shade in sunlight. In uncoursed and rough-coursed walls the mortar makes little visual impact because of the cobbles' projection and the way they are set to nestle closely to each other. By contrast, in coursed walls, owing to their rounded shapes and the clear separation of adjacent courses, much more mortar shows between the flints and between the courses. Galleting, however, is rare in cobble walls and such occasional instances as may occur are more likely to be found in inferior coursed work in which the cobbles have little projection, or where they have been partially buried by later excessive pointing. There are one or two examples from the late nineteenth or early twentieth century in the neighbourhood of Aylmerton (14) and Felbrigg.

In uncoursed walls there may be considerable variation in the size and shape of the cobbles; but in coursed and rough-coursed work they are more uniform in size and, on the whole, of more regular shape. The impression created by an evenly-laid coursed cobble wall has been aptly likened to plain knitting (27). However, where the courses impinge more closely on each other and the cobbles are more tightly packed, as on the Victorian tower of Woolpit church, the coursing is barely noticeable. There are countless examples of such walls, particularly in Norfolk, the best of the coursed work being found mainly in the coastal villages.

Pebbles may be laid coursed or uncoursed, the latter arangement being the most common. In the finest examples of this technique the pebbles are set with about half their body proud from the backing and so closely adjacent that no mortar is visible, and when selected for uniformity, eggshell smoothness and freedom from fracture or blemish, pebbles laid in this way create textures of bewitching appeal. Walls of this kind differ in their construction from traditionally built cobble walls in that the pebbles are laid as a facing set into a mortar rendering that has been applied to the surface of the backing wall. It is only by such means that decoration of the kind seen on the gable of Overstrand School (28) can be achieved.

Relying essentially on smooth uniform pebbles, as it does, it is to be expected that this type of work will be found mostly at or near the coast; but being a comparatively expensive labour-intensive technique it is not particularly common. There are fine traditional examples in Sheringham, Cley next the Sea and Holt, where one charming terrace of nineteenth-century cottages has uncoursed pebbles on the street elevation and rather erratically coursed cobbles on the end wall. Recalling this tradition, the precast concrete panels faced with uncoursed, closely-set even-sized grey pebbles which clad the window bays of the modern flats in Sheringham (13) that have been referred to, demonstrate an expressive contemporary use of pebbles – a good example of a local tradition interpreted in modern terms.

Pebbles laid coursed are less common. The Methodist chapel in Dersingham, of 1878, is a colourful example where pebble flints keep company with sea-worn pebbles of dark brown carstone and Hunstanton Red Rock. Sadly, the latter have not weathered well and are disintegrating. The appearance of this particular wall suggests that it was built in the traditional manner rather than by the applied facing technique.

CHAPTER SEVEN

Knapped Flint

CLEFT RUBBLE

The essential characteristic of all knapped flintwork is that each piece of flint has a cut surface exposing the flint core. Cleft rubble is its crudest form, the cut flint faces having been roughly chopped rather than skilfully knapped. The pieces vary in size and show little, if any, sign of trimming to regular shapes. They may be of any colouring and laid in any coursing mode, galleted or ungalleted.

Walls of this material can look very different from one another. At one extreme, relatively small pieces, their sectioned profiles often revealing the tortuous shapes of the nodules from which they were cleft, may be randomly laid quite closely to give a small-scale busy texture. At the other, large pieces may be widely spaced and show large expanses of mortar. Between these extremes come many walls composed of roughly cut flints of different shapes and sizes.

Although this kind of walling looks fairly crude, and some medieval examples are very rough indeed, the fact that face material involving the extra labour of cutting was used at all suggests that its builders considered that even the coarsest split flint was superior aesthetically or in prestige to the natural material.

The late-thirteenth-century chancel south wall of Great Barton church (29) shows an early use of cleft rubble: the uncoursed flints are closely packed and their varied sizes and rather angular untrimmed shapes create a typical rugged surface texture. Surprisingly, strikingly similar walls are seen on many nineteenth-century cottages and farm buildings, demonstrating that this particular technique possesses a timeless inevitability. A contrasting manner is seen on a nineteenth-century cottage group in Thornham (6) where the wide mortar gaps between coursed cleft flints are galleted with pebbles.

KNAPPED FRAGMENTS

Despite a superficial resemblance to natural ones, knapped fragments are the consequence of much more recent events: they are a by-product of the flint-knapping process, being the waste severed by the knappers during the reduction of virgin flints to the shapes and sizes that are required for better quality building material, or for the manufacture of gun-flints. As a result, at least part of the surface of each piece is exposed core, and the fracture edges are sharp by contrast with the softened edges of naturally broken ancient fragments.

As fragments, the pieces generally tend to be small. They are usually built uncoursed and a good interlocking fit is possible because of their predominantly angular rather than curved shapes. The surface of fragment-faced walls is mainly though not exclusively composed of the cut faces, and here and there parts of the original surface cortex show on some of the flints.

Understandably, this type of work is mostly found near centres of knapping, and in the Brandon area in particular there are several examples. These are usually confined to the side and rear walls of houses, a better quality of material being employed for the fronts. In this area, since they come direct from the chalk and are unstained by ground pigments, the flints have white cortices, making the walls a medley of black and white.

Elsewhere, walls faced with this inferior material are not very common and it is likely therefore that most of it was used as interior wall filling, especially in buildings faced with knapped flint where the knapping had been executed at the building site.

SELECT

Regular knapped faces and simple undistorted outlines are the fundamentals of the components of 'knapped select' flintwork. It is described as 'select' because the range of flints is limited to those conforming to certain standards of size and shape, and although they may vary within limits in a wall or between different examples, they are of a consistent character. Their selection may be said to be for conformity rather than uniformity.

These flints are usually of simple round, oval or polygonal shapes, mainly with rounded corners and curved edges rather than straight, angular or contorted ones. Many are clean splits from cobbles and these often show the white line of the cortex round their edges, while others seem to have been partly or wholly trimmed to their final shapes. Their sizes vary within a limited and compatible range, but an average size in a typical wall may be about 14 cm (5.5 in). Larger or smaller sizes are seen in some walls although the determining feature in all of them is the consistency of scale of the flintwork. The flints are found in all the normal core colours, laid to all coursing patterns, and are both galleted and ungalleted.

This style of flintwork, which is seen at its earliest in the Roman walls of Burgh Castle (73), has graced buildings of quality from the fourteenth century onwards. It was frequently used in the famous Wool Churches of the Perpendicular period, in important secular buildings of later centuries and in many Victorian church restorations. As may be guessed, it comes in many different forms, and the following examples illustrate the wide differences in shape, coursing, colouring and galleting of this type of flintwork.

The fourteenth-century walls on the south side of Thompson church are representative of early knapped flint in which the individual pieces, although of different shapes, are judged to conform sufficiently in size and character to give the consistency of surface rhythm that is the hallmark of this style. They are nevertheless on the borderline between cleft rubble and select, and on another borderline in their coursing and galleting: rough alignments are noticeable here and there, but other parts are uncoursed and there is occasional galleting with flint flakes.

If from a distance, the walls of Southwold church appear plain grey and devoid of any coursing emphasis (118), close inspection shows that the flints are in fact carefully coursed. Their regular size, trimmed polygonal shapes and close setting, aided by a little discreet galleting, disguise the coursing and diminish the personalities of the individual flints to the extent that they simply become part of a seemingly monolithic wall, and their respective shades of brown, grey and black merge into a muted monochrome.

At nearby Blythburgh church, the flintwork is again coursed but it is neither rigidly trimmed nor closely fitted and so, unlike Southwold, each flint clearly displays its own special character. Although there is variation in the flint shapes, selection has been made for compatibility of size. The coursing, nevertheless, though regular and discernible, is not as emphatic as can be achieved with material of more uniform shape. The glory of Blythburgh's flintwork, however, is its colouring – the knapped faces of blue-grey, amber and light grey in a random blend create a delightful harmony of shades (30).

Ungalleted select-knapped flints that are laid widely spaced like those in most walls of the Victorian church at Booton create a rather severe impression because the amount of visible mortar is too obtrusive. By contrast, the same kind of work, but prolifically galleted with flint flakes, is much more lively, as the west wall of Norwich Guildhall (5) shows.

Modern usage of select-knapped flint can be seen in the precast concrete cladding panels on several commercial buildings in the centre of Thetford.

A refinement of select-knapped flint, which perhaps almost justifies a separate classification, is occasionally found in superior work. It is identifiable from the exquisite knapping and trimming of the individual flints and their careful selection and laying. The flints have unusually flat faces and their edges are impeccably trimmed to produce softened rectangular and ovoid outlines that are free of angularities. Generally laid coursed or rough-coursed, this kind of work relies on closeness of fit rather than galleting to minimize the visible mortar.

The south aisle wall of Debenham church (31) is a Victorian restoration but a more refined example of skilled craftsmanship in select-knapped flint is unlikely to be found anywhere. The flints are of a fairly uniform size, mainly more or less oval or polygonal with softened corners, and fitted to each other with such artistry that the mortar is virtually invisible: there is certainly no need for galleting here. The flint colours are a perfect harmony of blue-black, blue-grey, light blue and white, and characteristic of the early stages of recortication of the knapped faces.

The same superb quality of workmanship but with a darker colour balance occurs on the west wall of the fifteenth-century porch of Ardleigh church, where it is laid rough-coursed, even if with marked horizontality, and there is similar flintwork and coursing on the south aisle wall of St Mary's church, Bungay (32), with flints in shades of blue, grey, and amber and occasional small pieces of buff limestone.

OVALS

A style of flintwork popular during the nineteenth and early twentieth centuries that is particularly, but not exclusively, prevalent in the coastal resorts of Norfolk, is one in which all the flints have been knapped and come in neat oval shapes.

At the coast, the beaches provided a plentiful supply of evenly rounded cobbles which, when cleanly split, yielded the knapped face and simple oval profile required for this work; but at places inland where no such amenable material was available, the ovals were prepared from irregular-shaped flints which had to be hand-trimmed to an oval shape after their initial splitting. It is sometimes possible to tell the difference between the two types because on cobble-derived ovals, apart from those from decorticated flints, the white cortex line around their edges may be evident. Trimmed types do not show a cortex line although on some there may be an incipient whitening of their chipped edges where cortication has started its inexorable creeping advance.

When they are laid uncoursed, size variations in the pieces are of advantage in minimizing the amount of exposed mortar, but however closely the flints are set, their oval shapes inevitably leave small visible gaps.

There are a number of buildings with flintwork of this type at coastal places in Norfolk, particularly in Sheringham. Also in Sheringham, there are examples, probably dating from the early twentieth century, in which each oval is meticulously ringed with thin wafers of white flint galleting that form a lace-like filigree lively with sparkle and radiance (33). Incongruously, this superb artistry is displayed on otherwise rather unexceptional villas.

Where ovals are laid coursed, it is clearly necessary that they should be graded for uniformity of size, at least within a particular course. In practice, in coursed work, the smaller ovals are usually laid with their long axis set vertically, or nearly so; this means that the larger ones, through their being set at an angle, can be accommodated without distortion of the coursing.

The finest craftsmanship in coursed work using hand-shaped as opposed to split-cobble ovals is to be seen, it need hardly be said, at Brandon where this and other sophisticated techniques appear on several nineteenth-century houses and cottages in the town (34). Not far from another flint-knapping centre, Norwich, the immaculately coursed ovals of the tower of Kirstead church, built in 1864, also appear to be largely hand-trimmed. These are noticeably uniform and include a generous proportion of almost circular pieces; most of the oval ones are laid lengthways. At Brandon and Kirstead the flints are black and grey, but on the north vestry of Aldeburgh church and in the panels below the west transept windows of Leiston church (35), similar material is mainly of brown and amber shades, with many of the flints showing concentric tone variations.

Knapped ovals are a special form of knapped flint, and where all the flints in a wall are of good oval shape, there is no difficulty with identification. However, in a case where a number of the flints are less than perfect in shape but nevertheless have a curved perimeter with no angularity, it will be a matter of judgement whether the flintwork merits this classification or whether it is simply select.

SCALES

The name given to this type of flintwork only describes its superficial appearance and is in no sense indicative of the structure of the material or the way it is laid.

Built conventionally and laid uncoursed without galleting, the flints are similar to ovals, but parts of the perimeter of some of them are knapped to a concave profile so as to embrace the convex curvature of adjacent ones, thus minimizing the impact of the mortar and creating a pattern which gives the impression of overlapping – and is reminiscent of fish scales. It is interesting to speculate whether this resemblance was a deliberately sought effect or simply the fortuituous outcome of a craftsman's search for perfection in fit and the elimination of visible mortar. Whatever the original rationale may have been, a rare innovation was added to the vocabulary of East Anglian flintwork.

It is quite in keeping with the architectural spirit of the idiosyncratic church at Booton, built between 1875 and 1891 to the design of its rector, that an innovative style of flintwork should find expression there. Although most of its flintwork is rather ordinary, with a good deal of exposed mortar, the east end wall is enlivened by a delightful display of knapped flint laid in the scales manner (36).

There are one or two other examples on houses in Sheringham.

BLOCKS

Irrespective of the type of flintwork, the vast majority of flint walls convey the general impression of being compositions in which the individuality of the component parts is subservient to an overall textural effect. This is as much due to the small size of the components as to their forms, and one becomes subconsciously accustomed to accepting this small-scale texture as the norm. Hence, buildings whose flints are of fairly regular shapes and significantly bigger than usual tend to stand out as noticeably different.

In certain areas, for example towards the western limits of the Norfolk chalklands, unusually large flints are found. Trimmed into roughly rectangular blocks with knapped faces, they are laid evenly coursed, with those in adjacent courses arranged to 'break joint' to some extent so as almost to achieve the effect of bonding (37), as realized in masonry walls. The block sizes vary and may be up to about 30 cm long by 15 cm high (12 by 6 in), which gives an indication of the size of the original nodules from which they were shaped. The knapped faces may be any of the normal flint core colours and, because of their unusual size, the lighter shades may easily be confused with chalk.

The relatively even shapes of the blocks tend to expose less mortar in the joints than is the case with rougher material, but, all the same, flint or carstone galleting is not uncommon. Sometimes single lines of thin flint flakes delineate the bed and perpend joints, but in other cases the massing of flint gallets disguises rather than accentuates the rectangularity of the blocks.

This technique was probably not used before the nineteenth century.

ROUGH-SQUARED

Squaring is perhaps a too flattering description of the shaping process by which the components of rough-squared flintwork are fashioned; nevertheless, they convey a general impression of having undergone more purposeful trimming than in normal select work. Two distinct trends are noticeable: first, where the flints, however wayward their shapes, are four-sided with straight edges, and second, where they are trimmed to roughly rectangular shapes but are less angular and not necessarily straight-edged.

In the first type, the flints vary appreciably in size: some are half the size of this page, others no bigger than a matchbox, most of them lying between these limits. Owing to their generally straight outlines, they can be fitted closely to leave little mortar exposed; galleting is therefore usually unnecessary, and occasional small flints used to fill an irregular gap read more as part of the wall than as galleting. The variation in size of the pieces in this type of work is not conducive to formal coursing and so they are usually laid uncoursed or rough-coursed. Sometimes they are set in an uneven mosaic pattern like the sepia flint on Rackheath church tower (38).

The style goes back to the earlier days of medieval knapped flint, and examples from the fourteenth century appear in the walls of the Prior's Lodging at Castle Acre (39), where the flints are roughly coursed, and on the tower and chancel walls of Great Ellingham church, where they are uncoursed. At both these places they are mainly shades of grey, and weathering has recessed the joints so that the flints are left apparently unmortared like the stones of a dry-built wall. Similar flintwork in the clerestory walls of Wickmere church (40) from the same architectural period is of an almost pure whiteness, and at the opposite extreme stand the jet-black walls of nineteenth-century cottages in Brandon and Feltwell.

The flints of the other type are of a more uniform size, less sharply angular, and tend to have their top and bottom edges trimmed approximately straight. This allows regular coursing and is typical of the style that is well exemplified in the tower of Thrandeston church, particularly in its west and north walls, the south wall having lost much of its impact through later pointing. There, the coursed flints are mainly black and light grey and create an initial overall impression of being rectangular-shaped, though on close examination they are seen to be only crudely squared, to have rounded corners and curved edges, and furthermore to be quite heavily galleted. It is remarkable how these irregular shapes, when seen from only a short distance, manage to achieve such a distinct 'square' appearance.

SQUARED

Squared flintwork, sometimes called gauged, is unquestionably the most refined of all types of plain flint walling, demonstrating an assured mastery of the skills of both knapping and laying.

The pieces have well-cut true faces and are all knapped to accurate square or rectangular shapes and consistent sizes; they are almost always coursed and laid with such precision that no mortar is visible at the joints between the pieces or between the courses. Unlike other types of flint walling, the regularity of the material allows it to be laid with staggered perpends and this is often done, particularly in walls in which all the flints are square or nearly so and the courses are of regular height. There are, nevertheless, instances which suggest scant concern for scrupulous bonding. Flint sizes vary but typically are about 10 cm (4 in) square, and rectangular pieces are laid either lengthways or upright according to their size, but conform with course sizes established by the square pieces.

Squared flintwork attained its fullest flowering during the fifteenth century, contributing to the luxuriance of some of the Wool Churches. One of its earlier uses, though, is in the north wall of the Bridewell, Norwich, built as a private house in the late fourteenth century; some of its flints are unusually small, about 6 cm (2.5 in) square. But in East Anglia generally, squared flint for private houses has been used only rarely, notable examples being Beeston Hall of 1786, and Cromer Hall of 1827, both built in the Gothick style.

All hues of flint are represented in squared flintwork and the following few examples from medieval to modern times indicate some of the colours to be seen.

The Bridewell flints are the brownish black typical of the knapped flintwork of many of Norwich's medieval churches. By contrast, the south wall of the porch of Blythburgh church (41) provides a beautiful illustration of the blue-grey tone harmony so characteristic of lightly-corticated knapped flint: a few flints showing amber patches amidst blues and greys add a touch of variety and the charm of the work is further enhanced by rather less than accurate coursing.

Grey flint of a different mood – a sombre monochrome reminiscent of gault brick – is much used on Cromer church. It is knapped with flawless precision and impeccably coursed and bonded, and the courses of varying heights incorporate many rectangular pieces. Surprisingly, certain walls of this church, laid with equal precision, are of quite a different colour and introduce warmer chocolate-brown tones mottled with white and pink (42).

Mainly white flints, flecked with yellow and interspersed with some light greys, give a bright and fresh effect in the walls of an early-twentieth-century house in Upper Shering-ham, now a nursing home. The coursing is very uniform and all the pieces are square but laid with small gaps showing a little mortar between, which, being a matching tone, does not detract from the general appearance.

A nineteenth-century inn in Feltwell has the characteristic jet-black flints of the area, but they are not squared with great accuracy and the light mortar in which they are set is rather too assertive. However, they course well with the building's light buff-grey brick dressings which make an effective contrast to the black flints.

FLAKES

This curious innovation of the early twentieth century (sometimes confusingly called galleting) differs from most flintwork in that the material forms no part of the structure of the wall but is simply an overall facing applied to the surface.

It consists of small flakes of flint, no more than about 5 cm (2 in) long, struck from larger flints – probably the waste from knapping. The flakes are entirely of flint core material, mainly in white and grey shades which create an impression of light grey when seen en masse. The whiteness is due to incipient cortication to which all the cut faces of each small piece are prone.

Application of these small flakes to a wall was clearly a very labour-intensive operation. The backing wall would first have been rendered and then the flint flakes would have been individually pressed into the rendering before it set. Each small piece is set edgeways, and all are skilfully interlocked and overlapped in a way that would have been impossible by any means other than hand-placing.

As well as the painstaking workmanship, careful examination also reveals fascinating variations in the directional flows of small areas of the work that are reminiscent of swirls on the surface of a pond rippled by a sudden, turbulent gust of wind. Sadly, these subtleties are lost if the wall is seen from any distance, when the general effect is hardly more interesting than pebble-dash. This is, no doubt, why the technique was only a short-lived fashion: it was soon appreciated that the aesthetic ends did not justify the toilsome means.

The technique can be seen at Overstrand (43, 44), West Runton and Crossdale Street.

CHAPTER EIGHT

Compound Flintwork

MIXED FLINT

This classification comprises as-found and knapped flint used together in combinations in the same wall. As both these categories embrace several flintwork types, there are inevitably many variations whose appearance depends mainly on three factors – the character of the knapped components, the extent of their presence within the mixture and the quality of the rubble or cobbles with which they are associated.

Although rubble flint walls often contain broken flints, judging by their random disposition and the irregular nature of their fractures, they do not seem to be part of a coherent design pattern for the wall surface. In a mixed flint wall, however, inclusion amongst the as-found material of well-cut pieces as opposed to roughly broken ones, suggests an aspiration towards aesthetic refinement. The overall effect of the knapped flints is to produce walls with a rather flatter surface than in all-rubble work, the rubble components probably having been to some extent selected to exclude the more extreme shapes.

The distinction between mixed flint and flint rubble containing broken-faceted pieces can sometimes be rather tenuous. The essential difference is that in the former the exposed cores of the split pieces appear in the main to have been purposefully knapped to give flat faces, whereas in the latter the cleft faces look haphazard or accidental. In these cases, therefore, differentiation between the two types will depend on whether these flints are judged to be knapped or broken. Mixed flint may also contain non-flint erratics and, while one or two do not materially affect the appearance of a wall, a larger proportion tends to blur the distinction between this type and flint with stone erratics.

Since the late thirteenth century, countless walls of mixed flintwork have been built that consist of rubble, cobbles and knapped flint, coursed and uncoursed, galleted and un-galleted. In the east wall of the chancel of Great Barton church which was probably one of the earliest buildings to use mixed flint, about three-quarters of the material is cleft flints, the rest being rubble. Another common combination of the fourteenth and fifteenth centuries was knapped flint with cobbles; but the proportions and colours of the ingredients within such mixes can produce markedly different effects, as is shown by a comparison of, say, the walls of Thurne church tower (45) and the clerestory walls at Holt (46).

One particularly prevalent combination of material which seemed almost to become a standard style in the fourteenth, fifteenth and sixteenth centuries comprised knapped flints and unbroken cobbles, roughly two-thirds knapped and one-third whole flints, of a fairly uniform size and regularly coursed, but quite widely spaced and usually galleted with flint flakes. The richly galleted walls of Northrepps church and Baconsthorpe Castle (47) are typical examples of this favoured mix. In similar but ungalleted work on the side walls of the porch of Great Witchingham church, carefully selected flints are more closely spaced and a subtle pattern is created by differing shades of flint colour in dark grey, light grey and amber. These simple and beautiful examples epitomize the craftsman's delight in and understanding for his material.

The curious mixed flint of some early-twentieth-century houses at Glandford (48) illustrates the difficulty of differentiating between pieces of walling flint and galleting that results from an even gradation of the material from large to small. However, these walls have a flatness of surface that suggests that they may have been built against shuttering boards, in which case, can the smaller pieces legitimately be called galleting? The even gradation and random mixture of fragments, cobbles and large, blue knapped flints also has the effect of disguising an underlying rough coursing.

DECORATIVE COMBINATIONS

Considered in the light of the ornamental inventiveness displayed by East Anglian craftsmen using flint with other materials, it is surprising that the decorative possibilities offered by contrasting types of flint alone were not exploited more often than they were. There seem to be only a few decorative themes which rely on the colour and textural differences obtainable from flint in its different forms, and these are comparative rarities. Maybe the reason is that fourteenth-century endeavours in this direction were soon overtaken by a universal enthusiasm for flushwork.

The north aisle of Burstall church (15), which probably dates from the mid-fourteenth century, may well be the earliest instance where two different types of flintwork were separately used in the same wall to create a deliberate decorative effect. The aisle north wall, containing three pointed windows and a doorway, has three stages separated horizontally by moulded string courses at cill and arch springer levels. The panels of walling between and beyond the windows, about 2 m (6.5 ft) square, are faced alternately with light-coloured rubble flint and dark knapped flint; above the upper string course, proportionate areas of these two flintwork types are shaped to conform with the curvature of the window arches and alternate with the panels beneath and the corresponding ones above, forming a primitive large-scale patchwork over the whole wall surface.

15 Alternating areas of rubble and knapped flints form a large-scale patchwork
     on the fourteenth-century north aisle of Burstall church

Simple, paired panels with foliated heads introduce a singular and unfamiliar style of decoration on the fourteenth-century upper stage of Kedington church tower (*106*). The panels are executed in contrasting black knapped flint set flush with the flint rubble wall surface, and, except where they are alongside quoins, they make a straight joint to the walling rubble without any form of margin. They have flush freestone heads and probably originally had flush freestone 'mullions' between them, though these are now mainly renewed in brick. The paired panel motifs appear in three faces of the tower, twice in the west and south walls and once in the east, and in each face their positioning is a little different.

Great Ellingham church, from the same architectural period as Burstall, has an early example of a chequer pattern comprising squares of neatly knapped and squared flints that alternate with squares of rubble flint with erratics (*49*). This pattern is quite extensive and covers the clerestory, the top stage of the three-stage north and south chancel walls, and the middle stage of the east wall. The textural contrast between the two flint types is augmented by their colour differences – the knapped squares are mainly blue-black whereas the rubble squares are yellowish-brown. Except on the east wall, where they are a little smaller, the chequer panels are about 30 cm (1 ft) square. Unfortunately, much of the chequerwork has been repointed to the extent that the rubble squares have almost been

16 Knapped flint squares and
voussoirs within the coursed
rubble flint wall of the
fourteenth-century belfry
stage of the round tower
of Syleham church

obliterated and now have a rendered appearance; but at the time of writing, the south wall
of the chancel has escaped such treatment. The tower buttresses echo this theme with
alternating panels of knapped and rubble flint on their outside faces between freestone
quoins.

Great Ellingham must be the most important example of two-type flint chequer decoration. There are minor examples elsewhere such as the fifteenth-century parapet of the
round tower of Haddiscoe church and the curious margins of knapped squares within a
rubble wall around the belfry openings and base of the upper stage of the round tower of
Syleham church (16).

The textural contrast between rubble and knapped flints has occasionally been exploited
by means other than the chequer pattern: on the tower parapet of Little Waldingfield
church, the merlon and indent zones of the crenellations alternate with the two flint types

and are separated by stone strips in an elementary form of flushwork; and on the parapet of Dickleburgh tower, stone and knapped flint in chequers of nine squares alternate with foliated panels of uncoursed cobbles (50). There, the knapped squares of the chequer and the cobble panels are directly contiguous and consequently the effectiveness of the design is dependent on their colour and texture differences.

The restored chancel walls of Uggeshall church feature another type of flint patterning. At intervals of about 90 cm (3 ft) in a wall of uncoursed flint rubble, there are horizontal bands, 15 cm (6 in) high, of black knapped flints. Being untrimmed, their irregular shapes make little textural contrast with their background and so the impact of the pattern relies almost entirely on the tonal difference between the two types of flint. Two similar bands of knapped flints about 25 cm (9 in) wide and 3.6 m (12 ft) apart once encircled the early-fourteenth-century round tower of Cockley Cley church but, sadly, in August 1991 the tower fell down. However, about half its circumference remains standing to about nave ridge height and the banding can still be seen on this section. The anatomy of the wall as revealed by the collapse showed that the knapped flint banding was an integral part of the tower's wall construction and not a later insertion, thus proving a contemporary date for the tower and this unusual decoration. There are traces of comparable banding, though far less distinct, on the round tower at Tuttington; and at Edingthorpe rather irregular bands of knapped flint are just discernible in the tower's cobble flint fabric, although they provide little contrast to it.

Another theme is to be seen on the north porch of Claydon church, where in walls of coursed flintwork, single black knapped flints alternate with groups of two or three lighter-coloured cobbles, the knapped flints being positioned above the centre of the cobble groups of the preceding course. Despite quite a variation in the sizes of the black pieces, the general effect is of a consistent pattern; but unfortunately, strident modern pointing has all but buried the cobbles and stifled the pattern's rhythm.

A few knapped flints are sometimes incorporated within background walls of as-found material to form symbols or small decorative motifs. At Hemblington church, for instance (51), three crosses carefully executed in squared knapped flints are set in the rough rubble flint and brick wall of the porch. This style of decoration was also often used on secular buildings, being found in particular on the gables of seventeenth-century houses, usually in combination with brick. A typical design appears on the gable of a Norfolk house dated 1680 in a wall of coursed cobbles (81); there, the contrast between the lighter cobbles and the knapped flint is perhaps weaker now than it would have been before more than three centuries of cortication faded the faces of some of the knapped flints.

While the visual impact of all these themes depends on the difference in appearance of two sorts of flint, effective decoration has also been achieved with the use of different coloured flints of just one kind. On Beechamwell church tower, above two of the flushwork feigned belfry windows, knapped flints in shades of yellow, white and black make small decorative motifs in a mosaic style (52), and on the pebble-faced gable of the school at Overstrand (28), different-coloured pebbles, similar in size to those used in the wall, depict a date panel and founder's initials.

CHAPTER NINE

Flint with Brick

In addition to its traditional role as a material for quoins and dressings, brick is often used in the face of flint walls to assist in bonding the facing into the heart of the fabric, and, as a result of this functional need, a variety of aesthetic expressions have evolved.

RANDOM

In these varied and unpretentious arrangements of flint and brick, the description 'random' applies to the disposition of the bricks, which, because the strongest bonding is obtained from a brick when its length is built into a wall, more often show as headers, although stretchers are by no means a rarity.

Roman bricks used randomly amongst flint can be seen in many early churches, for example in the chancel walls at Barnardiston, and medieval bricks appear at random within the flint fabric of several fourteenth-century round church towers. Later, random bricks are commonplace in the flintwork of lesser buildings where they are often of poor quality, and on some nineteenth-century cottages in Thetford, large distorted lumps of kiln waste are used instead (53). The bricks are usually unevenly distributed, laid to no definite pattern and often haphazardly angled; the walls may be coursed or uncoursed, and, in coursed work, brick headers are often set on end or inclined (54) so as to match the height of the larger flints.

The flints may be of any kind: for example, rubble, like those in the frenzied brickwork of a cottage at South Creake (55); cobbles as in farm buildings at Bacton (78); mixed as in the wall of a late-eighteenth-century cottage at Cockley Cley (54); or knapped as in the walls of a house in Mundford (56).

CHEQUER

Chequer compositions, which are sometimes called chequerboard, comprise two materials laid in alternating square or rectangular panels to form a chessboard pattern. True chequers are distinguished by their relative geometric precision and the touching corners of adjacent panels, features that are not usual in the more freely disposed components of other alternating patterns.

Brick chequer is less common in East Anglia than in the more southern chalklands, particularly in vernacular buildings, and, where it does occur, knapped flints seem to have been preferred in the flint squares of the pattern.

When brick is one of the materials of any chequer design, the size of the panels is invariably established from the brick's dimensions; thus, the smallest practicable panel size derives from the width of a brick, as shown by the panels on the front of the porch of Hardwick church (57). There, 12.5 cm (5 in) brick squares consisting of two headers, one above the other, or half a brick set with its bed face outwards, alternate with single knapped flints trimmed to a square shape.

On Weybourne church porch (58) which uses red bricks and white flint, and on the chancel at Lawford where the bricks are pale and the flint black, the chequer panels are about 23 cm (9 in) square. This derives from the length of one brick and the height of four 5 cm (2 in) bricks. With thicker bricks in the chequer on the parapet of Saxlingham church tower, only three are needed to make squares of the same size. At New Buckenham (59), the squares on the tower parapet are larger: one-and-a-half bricks wide by five bricks high.

Rich red bricks and blue-grey knapped flints are the materials for the greatest tour-de-force of brick chequerwork – the tower of Wheatacre church (17, 60). From brick plinth to flint parapet, this astonishing sixteenth-century edifice is dramatically patterned with a large-scale flint and brick chequer. The panels, both square and rectangular, are up to 75 cm (2.5 ft) wide and 60 cm (2 ft) or more high. On the lower stage of the tower, they form a simple chessboard pattern, but above this, several of the brick panels are twice the height of the lower ones, thus increasing the complexity and eccentricity of this unique creation.

FLEMISH CHEQUER

The name given to this style arises from the similarity of its brick pattern to the pattern of headers in a solid brick wall built in Flemish bond. Flemish chequer is a close, small-scale pattern of coursed flint with brick headers in which the proportions of the two materials are about equal; every course contains brick headers regularly spaced about a brick's length apart, and staggered in relation to those in adjacent courses, with two or three flints between. Size variations in the material often cause the pattern to wander slightly from geometrical precision, an imperfection which enhances the visual appeal, as, for instance, in the gable of Stiffkey church porch.

17 Large chequer of knapped flint and brick on the sixteenth-century
tower of Wheatacre church

As in other patterns, the flints may be rubble, cobbles or knapped. Two nearby nineteenth-century houses in Great Massingham display Flemish chequer that uses different kinds of flints with brownish-red brick: one has white rubble flints and the other, darker, knapped flint. Unusually for this type of work, both are galleted, the former with flint pebbles and the latter with flint flakes. The same pattern on a house at Feltwell (*61*) makes a very different impact because there the bricks are the characteristic buffs of the area and the knapped flints are jet black. But for impressive spectacle in this style, nothing can rival the great thatched tithe barn at Herringfleet (*62, 63*) which, restored in 1652, probably dates from the previous century: above a diaper pattern in the lower part of its long south wall, light grey cobbles in ones and twos alternate with mellow red bricks in broad expanses of radiant chequerwork.

Flemish chequer also forms the framework in a rare practice seen on some walls of the alleys in Lowestoft known as 'scores' (*64*): these walls have flint pebbles between the brick headers and sometimes as many as ten pebbles, in two rows, are packed within the height of a normal brick course.

OPEN CHEQUER

This type of chequer comprises an arrangement of bricks within a coursed flint background in which the bricks, laid level, are distributed horizontally and vertically at regular intervals, with wider spacing than in Flemish chequer, to form an overall pattern. The bricks are normally headers and the flints may be of any type.

The scale of the patterns will vary according to the spacing of the bricks, to whether they are introduced into each course or alternate courses and to how they are vertically aligned. A common layout, and one which gives a well-balanced rhythm, has bricks in alternate courses only, the horizontal gaps between the bricks being about three times their width and the bricks in the rows above and below being aligned over the gaps. This spacing, with red headers within a black knapped flint background, is used on a late-seventeenth-century house in Methwold (*65*) and with buff bricks in herringbone pebbles on Bawdeswell church (*66*). Similar distribution occurs in the rubble flintwork of the twelve-sided parapet of the round tower of Brooke church where the pattern is formed with rare 23 cm (9 in) square bricks (*67*).

Many similar arrangements of bricks within flintwork lack precise alignments or consistent spacing of the bricks but nevertheless create loose chequer effects. Red bricks in a free open chequer of this kind provide colourful variegation to the walls of the fourteenth-century tower of Mattishall Burgh church, and imaginative modulations are used with unaffected artistry on the walls of a barn at Salthouse (*68*) where courses of brick headers and cobbles are separated by up to five courses containing cobbles only: this produces a series of related rhythms rather than one overall pattern. In such cases there may be fine distinctions between this type and Random or Morse. Essentially, free open chequers have a discernible, if uneven, rhythm.

MORSE

This distinctive coursed arrangement is a random variant of open chequer in which brick headers and stretchers alternate irregularly with groups of flints that consist exclusively of rounded cobbles or pebbles, with perhaps a few compatible nodules, all of which have been selected for their uniformity of size. The name derives from the characteristic dot and dash appearance arising from the intermittent spacing of round flints and flat bricks.

The bricks impose a uniform height for the courses and each course comprises groups of flint cobbles and bricks with varied spacing; occasionally the bricks are contiguous, but usually they have flints between – a single cobble or as many as ten – although on average the overall proportion of cobbles to bricks is about three or four to one.

The technique shows to best effect when the cobbles are the well-rounded water-worn kind and both materials have a bold projection from the mortar, as in the illustrated example from farm buildings near Bessingham (69). In this case, although plenty of mortar is visible, it is not unduly obtrusive because of the prominence of the bricks and cobbles. By contrast, on a farm building at Shouldham (70) the effect is less emphatic because both materials have little projection, the tonal differences between flint and brick are more subdued, and the joints are accentuated with carstone galleting.

DIAPER

The inspiration for most repetitive brick decoration occurring in flintwork can be traced to patterns made with bricks of a different colour found in walls that are built entirely of brick. This is certainly true of diaper designs for which there are fifteenth-century precedents, although it was during the Tudor and Elizabethan periods and the early seventeenth century that the diaper pattern was most fashionable, as typified in the brick-work of Kirstead Hall of 1614.

Diaper designs in flintwork, variously referred to as diamond, lozenge, trellis and lattice, are diagonal patterns on the wall surface with brick headers in successive courses over-lapping each other by about half their width to create a series of interlocking diamond shapes. The flintwork of walls bearing this pattern is usually coursed to coincide with the bricks and is generally knapped flint or selected cobbles, though occasionally, as on the east wall of Spexhall church dated 1713, rubble flint roughly coursed may form the back-ground.

An unusual application of diaper pattern appears on the clerestory of Great Witching-ham church (71), although its extent is limited by the small areas between the windows. The pattern, of red brick within a background of select grey knapped flint, extends only up to the level of the window-arch springings, above which brick headers are freely disposed in flintwork that is more noticeably galleted than within the lattice. This is perhaps one of the earliest instances of diaper pattern in flintwork, the clerestory probably being of the late-fifteenth or early-sixteenth century. At Burgh St Peter there is similar work of about the same date on the base of the church tower, whose enigmatic upper stages are of later provenance.

A small house of uncertain date at Felmingham has a most unusual front wall in which the western part (except for its cobble plinth) is faced with oval knapped flints within a diaper pattern of red bricks (72), whereas the eastern part, also with a cobble plinth, is wholly of red brick with a similar pattern of blue headers. Thus the façade displays the same pattern in two different media. Despite evidence of alterations, the wall gives the general impression of having been built as a unit even if the diaper bricks in the flintwork are thinner than those in the east end. The quality of the knapped flint is superb, with selected even-sized ovals coursing neatly with the bricks. A similar pattern using buff bricks appears on a nineteenth-century estate house in Oxborough.

The diamonds of the diaper pattern in the lower part of the south wall of the thatched barn at Herringfleet (63) are formed with red bricks; they are infilled with cobbles, or more correctly, partly infilled, because buff and brown bricks are also introduced into them – in a totally random manner; they appear to fulfil no aesthetic purpose other than softening the geometry of the pattern.

A variation of diaper design that is sometimes seen consists of brick diamonds set one above the other in single vertical rows, each vertical row being separated from the next by a gap of about the same width as the diamonds. There is an example on the coursed cobble gable of a farmhouse at Letheringsett.

BANDING

Banding is a constructional style in which single or multiple courses of bricks are laid in a flint wall at intervals, not only for decorative reasons but for the structural purpose of tying back the facing into the body of the wall. East Anglian precedent for the technique goes back to the Roman walls of Burgh Castle (73), but it is not until the eleventh century at St Albans Cathedral, where retrieved Roman bricks were incorporated, laid in courses, that flint and brick banding again appeared. After that, in post-Norman medieval times it is not common.

One of the earliest instances of banded flint and medieval brick occurs on the west bay of the early-fourteenth-century chancel of Lawford church where triple courses of buff bricks alternate with coursed knapped flints in bands of the same depth. From later in the same century, the crumbling tower of the ruined Stanway church (in Colchester Zoo) (74) and the crenellated parapets of the gatehouse towers of Wingfield Castle have single courses of red medieval bricks alternating with cobbly rubble flints. Similar materials are used in the same way on the fifteenth-century porch of Little Waldingfield church (75), on parts of which Roman tegulae fulfil the role of the bricks.

The lustrous surfaces of knapped flint associate particularly well with the weathered texture of medieval brick and their cooler tones complement the warmth of brickwork hues. A harmonious balance between these two materials is nowhere better shown than

continued on page 87

1 Flint nodules in the chalk cliffs at Weybourne

2 Putlog hole framed and bridged with medieval bricks in a fourteenth-century rubble flint wall

3 Dual coursing. Alternating courses of large and small material in parts of the tower walls of Elmswell church

4 Layer coursing of flints in the late-thirteenth-century walls of the round tower of East Walton church

5 Massed galleting of flint flakes in the early-fifteenth-century knapped flint west wall of Norwich Guildhall

6 Pebble galleting in a cleft rubble flint wall of nineteenth-century cottages in Thornham

7 Galleting with brick fragments in a farmyard wall of mixed flint, brick and chalk at Foulden

8 Carstone galleting in a wall of coursed flint rubble selected for uniformity of size, in a nineteenth-century house at Stoke Ferry

9 Blind arcading formed in rubble flintwork in the eleventh-century round church tower at Tasburgh

11 Medieval brick quoins and a flint and brick arch in the fourteenth-century tower of North Cove church

10 Roman brick quoins on the Norman chancel of High Easter church

12 Medieval brick and cut flint quoins on the sixteenth-century porch of Hempstead church

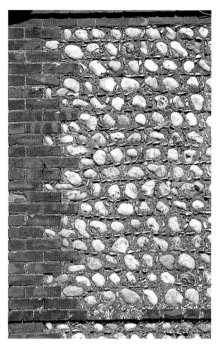

13 Alternating brick headers and stretchers at the window jambs and in the indented arch, in the flint rubble wall of a nineteenth-century cottage at Littlebury

14 Coursed cobbles galleted with flint flakes on an early-twentieth-century house at Aylmerton

15 Quoins, voussoirs and rustication formed with flint nodules in the Triumphal Arch at Holkham, designed by William Kent, c.1730

16 Rustication formed with flint nodules framed with animal bones on a small nineteenth-century house in Cley next the Sea

17 Prototype brick arch pattern on the fourteenth-century church tower at Market Weston

18 Mature brick and knapped flint arches of fifteenth century at Stiffkey church

19 A variation of the typical fifteenth-century arch, using pairs of bricks with knapped flints between. Badwell Ash church porch

20 Brick and stone voussoirs alternating with knapped flint in a window arch on the fifteenth-century tower of Hemingstone church

21 Cobbly rubble flint, roughly
coursed, subdivided by brickwork
members on an early-twentieth-
century cottage at Feltwell

22 Flint nodules of amorphous shapes in the late-
thirteenth-century chancel walls of West Harling
church

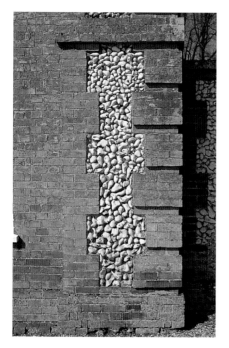

23 Uncoursed flint nodules selected for
the perfection of their white cortex.
The East Lodges at East Raynham,
1925

24 Uncoursed natural flint fragments on a nineteenth-century
house in Bramfield. Note the indented brick window arch

25 Uncoursed cobbles of strong orange shades, typical of the locality, on a nineteenth-century cottage at Whissonsett

26 Uncoursed cobbles on a nineteenth-century cottage at Langham

27 Coursed cobbles on a house in Trunch, *c.* 1600

28 Selected uncoursed pebbles on the village school at Overstrand

29 An early example of the exclusive use of cleft-rubble flint walling, on the late-thirteenth-century chancel of Great Barton church

30 Blue-grey, white and amber shades of coursed select-knapped flint in the fifteenth-century walls of Blythburgh church

31 Uncoursed, polygonally shaped select-knapped flint of beautiful blue-grey shades in the nineteenth-century south aisle wall of Debenham church

32 Refined select-knapped flint with occasional limestone in the south aisle wall of St Mary's church, Bungay. Probably eighteenth century

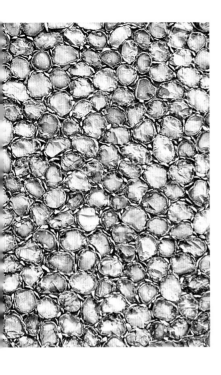

33 Uncoursed knapped
ovals with a delicate
galleting of flint flakes
in the walls of an early-
twentieth-century villa
in Sheringham

34 Meticulously knapped
ovals laid coursed on
a house in Brandon

35 Uncoursed knapped ovals, mainly in
brown shades, in part of the south wall
of the nineteenth-century church at Leiston

36 Knapped scales on the east wall of Booton
church. Late nineteenth century

37 Coursed knapped-flint blocks galleted with carstone chips on nineteenth-century cottages near Hillington. The blocks average about 13 cm (5 in) in height

39 Knapped and roughly squared flintwork of the fourteenth century on the Prior's Lodging at Castle Acre Priory

38 Roughly-squared flints of varying sizes laid in a mosaic pattern on the fourteenth-century church tower at Rackheath

40 Roughly-squared white knapped flints in the clerestory walls of Wickmere church, with inset flushwork cross botoné

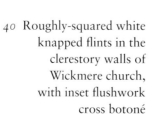

41 Squared knapped flint on the fifteenth-century porch of Blythburgh church

42 Squared knapped flint in chocolate brown shades on the side walls of Cromer church

43 Flint flakes on an early-twentieth-century house in Overstrand

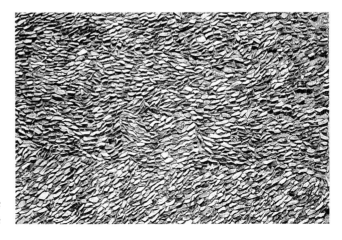

44 Close-up of the flint flake wall finish on the early-twentieth-century Overstrand house

45 Mixed flint, cobbles and knapped, in the fourteenth-century tower walls of Thurne church

46 Mixed flint with orange cobbles and white knapped flint in the fifteenth-century clerestory of Holt church

47 Knapped flint and cobbles laid coursed in the late-fifteenth-century east range of Baconsthorpe Castle

48 Mixed flintwork of knapped and rubble flint in early-twentieth-century houses at Glandford

49 Chequer formed with alternating squares of knapped and rubble flints on the fourteenth-century chancel of Great Ellingham church

o Stone and knapped-flint chequers alternate with foliated panels of cobbles in the parapet of an uncertain date on the fourteenth-century tower of Dickleburgh church

51 A cross formed in knapped flint within rubble on the fifteenth-century porch of Hemblington church

52 A motif in coloured knapped flints surmounts a flushwork imitation window in the fifteenth-century octagonal belfry of the eleventh-century round church tower at Beechamwell

53 Brick kiln waste with rubble flint
in nineteenth-century cottage
walls in Thetford

54 Cleft and rubble flints with random brick headers laid
sloping and roughly coursed in a cottage wall dated
1792 at Cockley Cley

55 Random brick headers chaotically mixed with
rubble flint in a cottage wall in South Creake.
Probably nineteenth century

56 Random brick within knapped flint
in the walls of a house in Mundford

57 Knapped-flint and brick chequer on the front of Hardwick church porch, comprising half-brick squares and single squared flints

59 Knapped-flint and brick chequer with one-and-a-half-brick squares on the fifteenth-century tower parapet of New Buckenham church

60 Detail of the large chequer of knapped flint and brick on the sixteenth-century tower of Wheatacre church

58 Light knapped flints and red bricks in a one-brick size chequer on Weybourne church porch

62 Flemish chequer of brick headers and flint cobbles above a diaper pattern on the seventeenth-century (or earlier) thatched tithe barn at Herringfleet

61 Flemish chequer formed with buff brick headers and black knapped flint on a nineteenth-century house in Feltwell

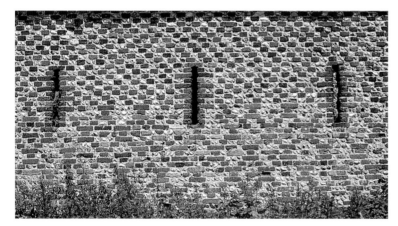

63 Detail of the Flemish chequer and diaper patterns on the walls of the tithe barn at Herringfleet

64 Flemish chequer with pebble flints in Crown Score walls, Lowestoft. Some courses have two rows of pebbles within the height of one brick course

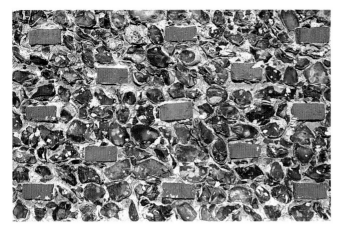

65 Open chequer of red brick headers in rough-coursed knapped flint on a late-seventeenth-century house in Methwold

66 Open-chequer pattern of brick headers in a wall of selected small cobbles laid in herringbone fashion on the modern church at Bawdeswell

67 Square bricks laid in an open-chequer pattern in the polygonal parapet on the round tower of Brooke church

68 Free open chequers of red brick in the coursed flint-cobble wall of a barn in Salthouse

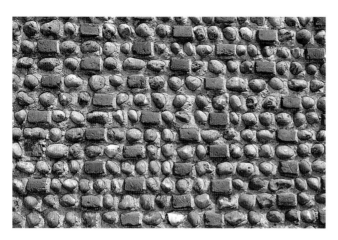

69 Coursed flint cobbles and brick headers laid in morse pattern in a nineteenth-century farm building near Bessingham

70 Morse pattern with cobbles and bricks, galleted with chips of carstone, on an eighteenth-century farm building in Shouldham

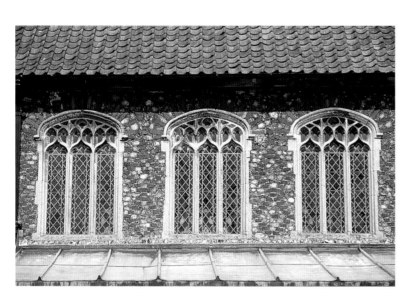

71 Brick diaper pattern on the fifteenth-century knapped-flint clerestory wall of Great Witchingham church

72 Knapped-flint ovals and a brick diaper pattern on the walls of a seventeenth-century house at Felmingham

73 Roman wall at Burgh Castle with select-knapped flint facing, reinforced with lacing courses of tegulae

74 Alternating courses of early medieval brick and flint in the ruined walls of Stanway church tower

75 Rubble flints alternating with courses of medieval bricks and Roman tegulae on the fifteenth-century porch of Little Waldingfield church

76 Alternating courses of medieval bricks and select-knapped flints in the fifteenth-century nave walls of Wicklewood church

77 Double-course brick bands, with black knapped flint between, over the entrance of the former Guildhall at Bury St Edmunds, with chequer flushwork in the parapet above

78 Brick header lacing courses in a flint cobble wall of a farm building at Bacton, Norfolk. Probably late eighteenth century

80 Double and triple courses of red tiles in intermittent and discontinuous lacing courses in the knapped flint walls of the nineteenth-century church at Radwinter

79 The chancel wall of Great Waldingfield church, rebuilt in 1866–9 to the design of William Butterfield

81 Date, initials and diamond patterns
in brick, in the flint-cobbled gable of
a Norfolk farmhouse

82 A brick cross within a diaper
pattern on a knapped flint background on the tower stair turret
at Little Massingham church.
Probably early sixteenth century

83 Brick patterns in the coursed cobble
flintwork gable of a farmhouse dated
1637, near Hunworth

84 Vertical bands of buff brick subdividing a wall of
mixed flint rubble and limestone at Weston Colville
church, rebuilt c.1825

85 Knapped flint and Hunstanton Red Rock (red chalk), galleted with flint, on a house at Holme next the Sea

86 Knapped flint and carstone conglomerate in an irregular chequer pattern in a seventeenth-century house wall in Old Hunstanton

87 Flint cobbles and brick-sized carstone blocks galleted with flint pebbles, laid in courses in the nineteenth-century chancel walls of Heacham church

88 Knapped flint and septaria at the Priory, St Osyth. Weathering has eroded the soft septaria, leaving the flints projecting

89 Occasional flints only amongst mainly non-flint cobble erratics in a nineteenth-century wall at Eltisley church

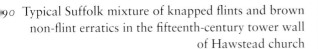

90 Typical Suffolk mixture of knapped flints and brown non-flint erratics in the fifteenth-century tower wall of Hawstead church

91 Knapped flint and limestone form a free check pattern in the fifteenth-century walls of Hilborough church tower

92 Cretaceous sandstone, probably from Lincolnshire, in the fifteenth-century tower walls of Reedham church. Compare with the limestone dressings

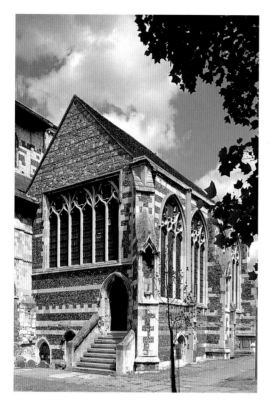

93 Flint and ashlar stone banding on the walls of the fourteenth-century south chapel of Waltham Abbey

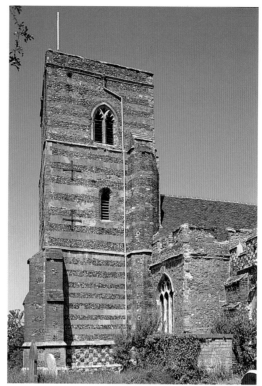

94 Alternating bands of knapped flints and rendered stonework on the fourteenth-century tower of Fingringhoe church

95 Knapped flint, cream limestone and buff and brown erratics create this attractive fifteenth-century coursed wall at Rickinghall Superior church

96 Gradual variation in the check pattern of knapped flint, limestone and erratics within the height of the north aisle wall of Great Barton church

97 Roughly-coursed knapped flint, limestone and brick in the colourful fifteenth-century clerestory of Ashill church

98 Pebble flints, limestone and brick in the chancel east wall of Theberton church

99 Rubble flint, brick and carstone, roughly coursed and galleted with carstone fragments, on a barn at Wereham, probably eighteenth century

100 Coursed flint, brick and carstone in a cottage wall in Fincham

101 Knapped flint, carstone and Hunstanton Red Rock in a colourful check pattern on the late-sixteenth-century parts of a farmhouse at Ringstead

102 Colourful mix of knapped flint, ferricrete, brick, and knapped non-flint erratics in the nineteenth-century walls of Ardleigh church

104 Seven different materials in the colourful fifteenth-century walls of Little Bentley church tower: flint, brick, crag, septaria, limestone, ferricrete and erratics

103 Flint, septaria and crag, with a few oddments of limestone in the nave walls of Salcott church

106 Prototype flushwork in the belfry stage of Kedington church tower. The lower stage, with its naive flower motif, was probably recased in the fifteenth century

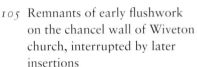

105 Remnants of early flushwork on the chancel wall of Wiveton church, interrupted by later insertions

107 Relief-carving motifs of the front parapet interpreted in flushwork on the side parapets of the fifteenth-century porch of Southwold church

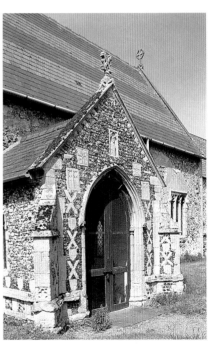

108 Various stone motifs inset within knapped flint backgrounds on the fifteenth-century porch at St Andrew's church, Barton Bendish

109 Knapped flint and limestone in a diagonal chequer pattern on the sixteenth-century porch of Walsham le Willows church

110 Straight and diagonal chequer flushwork on the porch walls of Stowlangtoft church

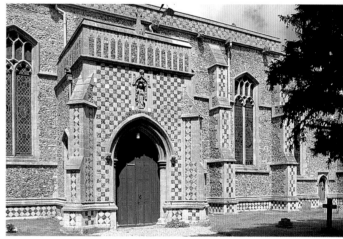

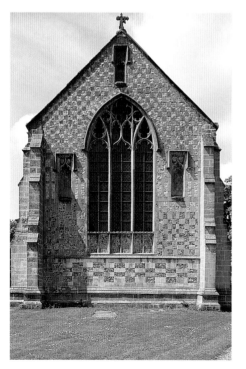

111 White knapped flint and limestone in straight chessboard chequer in the upper parts, and rectangular chequer of black knapped flint in the dado, on the fourteenth-century chancel east wall of Burnham Thorpe church

112 Knapped flint and limestone in lapped chequer pattern on the tower of St Mary's church, Luton

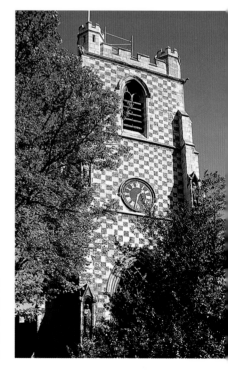

113 Replica window themes in flushwork under stone crocketed gablets on the fourteenth-century east wall remnant of Little Walsingham Priory church

114 Flushwork panelling echoing the window tracery, on the fifteenth-century south aisle of the church of St Michael at Coslany, Norwich

115 Flushwork rose window motifs in the pediments over the belfry openings, and panelled corner turrets, on the fifteenth-century church tower at Deopham

116 Flushwork panelling on the Priory Gatehouse at St Osyth

118 Three flushwork themes on the west front of Southwold church tower: chequer above the window, panelling each side and below, and serial flushwork of crowned Lombardic letters over the window arch

117 Flushwork chequer, panelling and circular motifs on the upper stage of St Lawrence's church tower, Ipswich, rebuilt in the nineteenth century

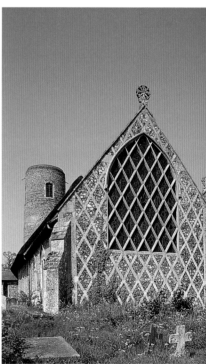

119 Paired flushwork panels with traceried, crocketed and finialled heads in the side walls of the fifteenth-century church porch at Glemsford

120 Unique flushwork panelling in an overall diagonal pattern continuous with the window mullions, on the chancel of Barsham church. Probably sixteenth century

121 Imitation window in medieval brick flushwork in the octagonal belfry stage of the round church tower of St Benedict's, Norwich

122 Late medieval brick flushwork panelling in the tower parapet of Caistor St Edmund church

123 Staggered panels of brick flushwork on the seventeenth-century parapet built on the medieval church tower of Ringsfield

124 Detail of the brick flushwork on the sixteenth-century brick porch at Great Ashfield church, showing moulded bricks in the panel heads

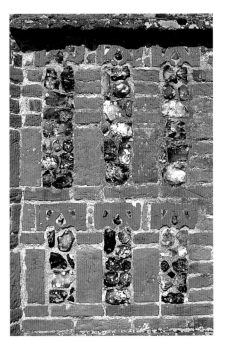

125 Proudwork parapet on Mattishall church tower. The moulded stonework stands proud of the knapped-flint infill of the quatrefoils and panels

126 Relief flushwork. Rubble flint as the infill material of the panelling on the base of Horham church tower

127 Relief flushwork of flint cobbles in the panelling on the church tower parapet at Sudbourne. This is probably a nineteenth-century or later restoration

128 Cobbles, mainly non-flints, form the relief flushwork in the lapped chequer walls of the nineteenth-century Papworth St Agnes church. All its walls are like this

18 Alternate courses of buff bricks and flint cobbles galleted with carstone chips,
    on a nineteenth-century cottage wall in Shouldham

in the fifteenth-century walls of Wicklewood church (76), where alternating courses of
shallow claret-red medieval bricks and lightly galleted knapped flints make a matchless
setting for the church's architectural stonework. The charm of this work lies not only in
the aesthetic relationship of the materials but also in the subtle difference in their course
heights, which frees the pattern from the risk of geometric rigidity. These walls are unique,
apart from small patches in similar materials on a tower buttress at Kedington church.

On the late-fifteenth-century porch of the former Guildhall at Bury St Edmunds (77),
double courses of red bricks alternate with black knapped flint. There, the flint bands are
a little wider than the brick and, as at Wicklewood, the slight dominance of one material
over the other gives this wall its pleasing architectural quality.

Alternating brick and cobble coursing, galleted with carstone, on the walls of a
nineteenth-century cottage at Shouldham (18) makes an interesting comparison with the
medieval precedents.

In lesser buildings of the eighteenth and nineteenth centuries, intermittent single or
multiple lacing courses of brick are sometimes built into flint walls, although this is not a
particularly common practice in East Anglia. Building-in the bricks in the patterns already
described seems to have been the preferred method of bonding a wall's facing into its body.

Nevertheless, lacing courses do occur in East Anglian walls, perhaps more usually on farm buildings and cottages. In such cases, unlike in the primarily decorative work at Wicklewood and Bury where plenty of stretchers appear on the face, the majority of bricks show as headers, thus expressing their structural role.

At Binham, a cottage gable is striped with single courses of red bricks between two or three consecutive courses of flint cobbles, and on farm buildings at Bacton, Norfolk (78), the materials are similar but the lacing courses are separated by seven or eight cobble courses. Similar spacing of red brick lacings is followed in the flint rubble wall of Baker's Row, a terrace of nineteenth-century cottages at Newmarket, and the same pattern in the so-called white bricks of the locality is seen again on a fine nineteenth-century barn and stables at Exning.

Roman tegulae form an encircling band around the battlemented parapet of the round tower of Pentlow church and are used plentifully in its merlons. They also occur in bands here and there in the nave walls at Great Waldingfield, and when rebuilding the chancel in 1866, the architect, William Butterfield, sought to reflect this style of work by incorporating a pattern of red tiles within cobbly rubble flintwork (79): although his regular tile-spacing gives the wall a rather mechanical rhythm compared with the freer arrangement in the medieval walls, it is an apt interpretation of the historical practice.

Plain tiles, as opposed to Roman tegulae, in the role of intermittent lacing courses are not common, however, in East Anglia. There are some in the cobble walls of a modern vestry at Cavendish church that are superficially reminiscent of the Roman work at Burgh Castle (73), but the most innovative association of plain tile banding with flint is to be seen in the walls of the Victorian church at Radwinter (80). The flintwork there is select knapped flint, mainly black, and the tiles are bright red: the tile courses, two and three tiles in height, are set within the flint partly as conventional lacing courses though chiefly as long and short discontinuous bands of random lengths at irregular spacings. This decorative system is incorporated in virtually all the walls of the church, including the tower.

FREE MOTIFS

By contrast with overall repetitive brick patterns, many traditional flint buildings display individual motifs depicted in brick against a coursed flint background. Dates and initials are the ones most frequently seen (81), but other themes popular with builders of the past include diamonds, hearts and chevrons, and larger motifs based on multiple combinations of these, often interlocked or inverted. All these designs rely almost entirely on diagonal lines of brick headers partially offset in successive courses, with stretchers only normally occurring where lines of headers intersect. Their style is therefore the legacy of a discipline imposed by the bricks. As the impact of the motifs depends on the contrast between brick and flint, it follows that this type of decoration is more usually carried out with red bricks rather than bricks of paler shades.

The late medieval stair turret of Little Massingham church (82), faced with knapped flint

19 Knapped flint decoration
   within the brick wall of
   the sixteenth-century
   rood-stair turret at
   Sustead church

and quoined with brick, bears a simple lozenge pattern within which is incorporated a
single cross symbol, the vertical continuity of the diamonds being interrupted to embrace
it. This is an early instance of an individual motif, though it is one that is not completely
independent of an overall pattern.

This style of decoration in its full maturity is well illustrated on a mid-seventeenth-
century farmhouse near Hunworth (83) whose coursed cobble walls carry several different
brick designs. Across the base of the south gable runs a 'meander' frieze, and above this the
gable peak bears a design based on concentric diamonds, which for the sheer size of an
individual motif probably has no equal elsewhere. Disposed informally in the spaces below

and between the windows on the front wall, hearts, diamonds, double chevrons and a wishbone can be identified amongst less determinate shapes.

A complete reversal of materials is seen at Sustead church where the rood stair turret is built in brick but incorporates flintwork decoration (19). Inverted chevron motifs and a cluster of diamonds are executed in white knapped flints that have been immaculately trimmed to the exact size and shape of brick headers and so merge to perfection with the brick coursing. Feeble echoes of this technique are often seen today in mediocre modern work where a few token flints set in brickwork pay lip service to the past but carry no conviction as a continuation of the flintwork vernacular.

At Kedington church (106) a brick motif within flintwork occurs in another form notable for its oddity. Unlike the rest of the walls, part of the east face of the tower between an earlier nave roofline and the tower's upper stage is faced with black knapped flint; set within this background is a flush stone panel in which a primitive five-petalled flower is depicted in bright red brick, the bricks also being inset flush. Reminiscent of a child's painting, this motif seems quite foreign to the Gothic decorative tradition.

FRAMING

In this type of architectural decoration which emerged in the eighteenth century and persisted through the nineteenth and into the early twentieth century, the surface of a flint wall is partitioned into smaller fields by horizontal and vertical strips of brickwork set flush with the wall face. Normally the bricks are of the same kind as those used for the quoins and the door and window jambs of the building.

The term 'framing' in this context is only used to express the frame-like appearance of the brick features and does not imply that they are a structural framework like traditional timber framing or the reinforced concrete and steel frames of modern buildings: the brickwork is simply an integral part of a weight-bearing wall, helping to bond the facing flints to the inner core of the wall, which in any case during the later nineteenth century and after may well have been of brick rather than flint. This role is affirmed by the high percentage of headers showing at the wall face.

Typically, the brick horizontals are aligned with a building's natural features such as window cills and heads, floor levels or eaves and are rarely more than three courses high. The verticals are usually positioned to extend the lines of doorway and window jambs, and they have indented edges to bond with the adjacent flint, sometimes at each course and sometimes at every three courses (21) – but usually continuing the bonding pattern used at the jambs.

A late Georgian house at Wixoe (20) with a two-storey three-bay frontage illustrates the orthodox disposition of the brick elements which, with little variation, became a pattern for many smaller houses. It has yellow bricks in its quoins and dressings and in the horizontal and vertical ribbons that subdivide the black knapped flint wall surface into separate rectangles. The horizontals are single brick courses laid level with the window-

20 Walls of black select-knapped flint, subdivided into separate fields by buff bricks, on a late Georgian house at Wixoe

heads, and the verticals are alternating single headers and stretchers; two full-height verticals divide the façade into three bays, with shorter verticals linking the jambs of the upper and lower windows to each other and to the brickwork of plinth and parapet.

To be visually effective, designs of this kind need some measure of contrast between the brick and the flintwork, but in some Suffolk towns, Sudbury for example, local buff-grey bricks are so similar in colour and tone to the natural flint that the patterns barely show.

Vertical brick bands are the basis of the curious pattern on the chancel and the tower of Weston Colville church (84), which were largely rebuilt in flint rubble and light buff brick in about 1825. Except for two platbands on the tower, there are no brick horizontals in the flintwork; and the main brick verticals on the chancel, comprising two stretchers alternating with three headers, take the form of upward extensions of the jamb dressings of the arched doorway and window openings. In addition to these, slightly wider single vertical bands are oddly located below the window cills.

CHAPTER TEN

Flint with Stone

FLINT AND CHALK

Although chalk is not a very suitable stone for external use in building because of its poor weathering qualities, it has been used to a certain extent, particularly in north-west Norfolk, and generally in conjunction with other materials.

Walls containing flint and chalk are usually of the rougher techniques and are found in lesser structures and farmyard walls rather than in buildings of quality. From a distance, the white chalk, typically appearing in rugged undressed lumps, is often difficult to differentiate from flint when the latter is of the rubble type with a white cortex or a split type showing a light face. Close inspection, however, reveals the different nature of the two materials: the chalk will be seen to have a soft granular surface in contrast to the firm crusty texture of a flint cortex or the hard gloss of a flint core.

Chalk seems to be more often used as one ingredient in walls of multiple materials and walls exclusively of flint and chalk are not particularly common: a few are to be found in the north and west parts of Norfolk, for example in Brancaster, where a cottage wall built of rough chalk lumps interspersed with white flint nodules, some showing fractured black cores, evokes the flint's primordial environment.

FLINT AND RED ROCK

Exposed in the face of the cliffs at Hunstanton and extending a little way inland, there is a bed about 1.2 m (4 ft) thick of rose-coloured rock between the white chalk above and the underlying brown carstone. The Hunstanton Red Rock, or red chalk as it is often called, although said to be harder than the white chalk, has not been much used for building except very locally, and usually in combination with other materials. A rare instance of the material on its own can be seen in part of the wall of a house near the church in Old Hunstanton; but elsewhere there and in one or two villages nearby it appears mostly in rough-looking walls mixed randomly with carstone, chalk, flints and bricks.

The Red Rock itself is used in irregular-shaped lumps, probably taken mainly from the beach as fallings from the cliffs, and in a wall with light-coloured mortar it is often almost impossible to pick out the individual pieces. In old walls particularly, the surfaces of the lumps are pitted and weathered up to the point of apparent disintegration and when laid in combination with flint, the effects of differential weathering on the two materials are quite conspicuous, the flints standing clearly proud from the rock.

These aspects are visible in a building in the village street of Holme next the Sea (85) dating perhaps from the seventeenth century, now converted into holiday cottages but probably formerly a single house: it has walls of Red Rock and knapped flint laid in regular courses and vigorously galleted with large flint chippings. The flints, grey to white in colour and compatibly sized, alternate in ones and twos with similarly spaced nodules of Red Rock to form a simple check pattern that is muted to some extent by the irregular shapes of the two materials and the galleting. Much of the mortar is virtually the same colour as the rock and so is lost in the overall texture of the wall.

Another beautiful example of knapped flint with Red Rock is to be found in the clere-story wall of Little Massingham church. This is remarkable on two counts, firstly for being probably a unique use of Red Rock in church building, and secondly for its distance from the likely source of the material, unless it came from a now unknown local outcrop. The coast is some fifteen miles distant, although the church is only a mile from the ancient Peddars Way which from Roman times ran from near Thetford to the coast at Holme next the Sea. The materials of this wall are the same as those on the house in Holme, but at Massingham the work is largely uncoursed and many of the flints are larger and less systematically laid. The galleting and the overall proportions of the two materials in the mix are similar.

The most arresting aspect of both these walls is, however, without any doubt, their colour: in full sunlight the glowing reds and pinks of the rock with the white sparkle of the flint make a memorable spectacle.

FLINT AND CARSTONE

Carstone is a ferruginous sandstone of the Cretaceous system; it lies below the Red Rock as can be seen in the cliffs at Hunstanton. In many shades of brown, from a fierce mustardy ginger to a deep purplish mahogany and often marked with black or purple veining, it outcrops along the west Norfolk escarpment between Hunstanton and Downham Market and here and there in a narrow band south-westwards. At a certain level in the Hunstanton cliffs the nature of the stone can be seen to change to that of a conglomerate, characterized by the presence of small pebbles that merge with the dark sandstone into a concrete-like coalescence, sometimes aptly called puddingstone.

Carstone and conglomerate have over many centuries been used for building in west Norfolk and they have been incorporated with flint in many ways, the contrast between dark stone and lighter flint being exploited to create simple patterns. Predictably, these combinations are characteristic features of north-west Norfolk.

The chancel walls of Wereham church are of uncoursed flint rubble containing about twenty per cent of small carstone nodules, hardly larger than the biggest flints; they are distributed randomly in such a way that no repetitive pattern is created but the wall is enlivened by textural and colour contrast. A house in Ringstead built of similar materials has reversed ratios of carstone and flint, which, by comparison with Wereham church, produce the impression of a photographic negative.

The gable of a seventeenth-century house in Old Hunstanton (86) faced with knapped flint and dark carstone conglomerate has a more deliberate pattern: the two materials are about the same size and evenly coursed, and in each course groups of two or three flints alternate with roughly-squared lumps of conglomerate that are aligned over the flint groups of the preceding course to form a Flemish chequer pattern.

The south side of Heacham church displays two assertive expressions of nineteenth-century showmanship in flint and carstone: the coursed chancel wall has groups of white flint cobbles alternating with carstone blocks galleted with little flint pebbles (87), while on the nave, patches of wall have been refaced in a strident irregular chequer of squared carstone blocks and white knapped flints, garnished with flint flake galleting. The same theme, though less insistent, also appears on cottage walls in Docking and Fring.

A more sensitive nineteenth-century combination of flint and carstone is seen in the restored south wall of Bessingham church nave. Echoing the ferricrete of the church's more ancient parts, chocolate-brown carstone rubble, randomly associated with blue-grey knapped flint, achieves an unusual but harmonious colour alliance.

Quite different in colour from the commonplace carstones, a cold grey stone, often with a slight olive cast, appears here and there at places within a few miles to the north and east of King's Lynn. Known as Silver Carr, it is evidently of local origin as its use for building is almost exclusively confined to this area although its actual source remains uncertain. The stone appears in vernacular applications as rubble or as small roughly squared blocks galleted with carstone on several houses and farm buildings in Hillington and other nearby villages; but it was also used in much earlier times. It is the main walling stone of the Norman keep of Castle Rising and, associated with flint, sizable lumps are roughly coursed with dark carstone in the lower parts of the round tower of Gayton Thorpe church, and quantities are also dispersed at random amongst flint rubble in the medieval walls of other local churches, most conspicuously in the chancel and tower at Hillington.

FLINT AND FERRICRETE

At places remote from the carstone outcrop along the west Norfolk escarpment, and indeed also in that locality, the walls of many early East Anglian churches contain a coarse stone that is similar in general appearance to carstone conglomerate but distinguishable from it by the angular or rounded fragments of flint held within its dark brown ferruginous matrix, which may also contain other pebble material. The presence of flint in its composition shows it to be geologically younger than carstone, and it is thought to come from localized deposits of consolidated gravels, naturally cemented by iron oxides. Geologically, it is probably quite recent.

This material has also been called puddingstone or gravelstone, but the term ferricrete now seems to be preferred by some geologists. It has been found fairly near to the ground surface, and has on occasion been unearthed by the plough; it seems that its distribution may be widespread though localized. Specific sources have not been identified and it has been suggested that the material may have been encountered fortuitously during excavations for flint. Wherever it appears in early church fabric, it is probably of local origin, as a coarse material such as this is unlikely to have been transported far from its source. It is found in church walls at various places in Norfolk, and in Essex in particular between the Stour and Colne estuaries.

Quite large pieces were often used for quoins in early flint churches and smaller lumps were disposed randomly amongst the flints in the fabric of ancient churches such as Shereford and Wickmere, or as quite distinct bands of walling as in the round church towers of Bessingham (3), Great Ryburgh and Roughton (21), where some courses near the base of the tower are laid in herringbone pattern.

FLINT AND SEPTARIA

Septaria is a clayey limestone laid down some fifty million years ago in the Eocene phase of the Tertiary period, and it occurs in a few places in coastal areas of north-east Essex and south-east Suffolk. It is a light- to medium-brown colour with a very coarse texture, and, exposed to the elements in buildings, the surface weathers erratically to give a craggy broken appearance.

Septaria was used locally for building by the Romans and then later at Colchester Castle and Orford Castle and in several churches near the Stour, Orwell and Deben estuaries. Its inferior weathering properties are strikingly demonstrated in the walls of Orford Castle keep where it has been weathered back 2.5 cm (1 in) or more behind the face of the limestone quoins and dressings.

In association with septaria, flint seems to have been limited mainly to rubble and cobbles in random mixes, as in the walls of such churches as Shottisham, Ramsholt or Kirton; but at St Osyth, the walls of the building immediately to the east of the Priory Gatehouse are a cheerful mixture of blue-black knapped flint and septaria (88, *116*). Here again, as at Orford, the septaria has been eroded to leave the flints standing sharply proud.

Also at St Osyth, there is a decorative combination of the two materials: a high wall surrounding the Priory grounds is built of septaria and at the top of its upper stage there are alternating panels of septaria and black knapped flint. The sides of the septaria panels

21 The Saxon round tower of Roughton church built with flint and ferricrete.
Note the alternating bands of ferricrete and flint, some laid in the herringbone
manner, near the base

are finished with dressed freestone, suggesting perhaps that the top of the wall was originally crenellated and the indents were later filled with flint.

FLINT AND CRAG

The Coralline Crag, deposited seven million years ago during the Pliocene phase of the Tertiary period, occurs in a small coastal area of Suffolk in the vicinity of Orford and Aldeburgh. It consists mainly of shelly sands, but occasional harder beds yield a buff-coloured stone which has been used locally to some extent, for example on Chillesford church tower and the chancel of Iken church.

Apart from its combination with black knapped flint in a loose open chequer pattern on the fifteenth-century tower of Salcott church and its imaginative use in the Victorian church at Leiston (see page 100), there seem to be few instances of Crag being used in association with flint other than randomly as an occasional ingredient in multi-material walls such as those of the churches at Little Bentley or Stoke by Nayland, for example, or as in the rather haphazard repairs to Orford church tower. It is also seen in mixtures with rubbly flint in boundary walls in this area.

FLINT AND STONE ERRATICS

The Quaternary period, variously estimated as covering the last one-and-a-half to three million years, saw marked climatic changes in the region, periods of intensely cold glacial conditions alternating with intervals of a milder climate. In successive glaciations, mantles of clays and sands containing flints and pieces of various rocks from as far afield as Scandinavia and Scotland, often worn and rounded in transit, were spread extensively over East Anglia by ice sheets as they moved across the area, and during the warmer inter-glacial phases, sands and gravels were deposited in floods and sea incursions caused by the melting land ice and associated changes in sea levels. It is these superficial deposits, known as Drift, which yield the random assortment of flints, non-flint cobbles and other stone erratics seen in buildings, churches in particular, in many parts of East Anglia.

The stone erratics may be almost any type of rock – igneous, metamorphic or sedimentary, and one or more different kinds may be present in the same wall. They are usually distinguishable from flint by their granular, crystalline or laminar natures, and their characteristics can have a marked effect on a building's appearance: they may vary from irregular rough-textured rocky lumps to smooth rounded cobbles or pebbles, and are mostly brown or buff shades with a few of crimson red. The flint components are commonly glacial boulders, nodules or other rubble forms and may represent greater or lesser proportions of the material in a mix; in some cases the ascendancy of non-flint cobbles, which in general are darker shades of brown than flints, is so complete as almost to displace flint from the make-up of a wall.

Usually laid uncoursed or rough-coursed, and often containing quite large pieces, walls of this kind are common in churches on the boulder clay and river terrace gravels of south Cambridgeshire, north-east Bedfordshire and north-west Essex, of which those at Eltisley (*89*), Eyeworth and Chrishall are typical.

Suffolk also has many churches with walls of flint and erratics, but the flint content there is usually greater than in Cambridgeshire and Bedfordshire. The tower of Hawstead church (*90*) shows a coursed mixture of mainly black or grey knapped flints and chocolate-brown erratics that is typical of many fifteenth-century Suffolk churches.

FLINT AND NON-INDIGENOUS STONE

Limestone is the most important variety of stone to be imported into East Anglia, and since Norman times it has been extensively used in conjunction with local flint. In church buildings, as ashlar, its principal external applications are in quoins, buttresses, plinths, parapets, sculpture, the dressings for doorways and windows, and of course as a constituent of flushwork. Nevertheless, it is also found as a component of flint walls, particularly in churches built during the great rebuilding period of the prosperous fifteenth century and in secular buildings built after the Dissolution of the monasteries. Stone salvaged from former structures, trimmed to roughly rectangular shape and showing a dressed face, found its way into flint walls, often being reduced to fairly small pieces comparable in size to the flints.

In uncoursed walls of flint and limestone, the distribution of the stone may be quite random, but where it is incorporated with coursed knapped flint, the stone, amounting to about a fifth of the material, is often evenly spaced, though without rigid precision, and forms a loose check pattern. Walls of this kind on the tower and porch of Hilborough church (*91*) have knapped flints with the attractive blue-grey shades of a lightly corticated surface which create such a pleasing harmony with the creamy greys of limestone. But at Thetford, where several buildings of the seventeenth century and later incorporate limestone fragments from the ruined priory and former churches, the walls lack the same appeal because the flints are dull, achromatic greys and black.

An unusual treatment in knapped flint and limestone occurs in a panel above the tower west window of St Mary's, Bungay, where the stone pieces, alternating with knapped flints to form a spotty check effect, are precisely circular: are they perhaps sections sawn from former stone shafts of earlier buildings on the site?

A different stone, possibly a Cretaceous Lincolnshire sandstone, appears with flint in an unusual arrangement in the walls of Reedham church tower (*92*). It is mainly a light blue-grey, with some pieces shading towards light olive, and consists of rectangular blocks that vary in size from about 20 cm (8 in) square up to about 45 by 30 cm (18 by 12 in). They are laid within a background of squared knapped flint of blue-black and grey shades and occupy about half the surface of the wall in relation to the flint, a balance which creates a lively but harmonious non-repetitive pattern. The differences in colour and texture between this stone and the limestone of the quoins and dressings are most striking.

An apparently similar stone, though rather pinker (possibly as a result of fire), is used for the north-west quoin of Brampton church. The roughly squared shapes of the quoin stones and the presence of Roman bricks in the lower part of the quoin suggest that they may be robbed walling from a Roman building.

Two other stones which each appear in a single church, need but a brief mention. At Colney, the north-west nave quoin, mainly of flints, contains a few rough blocks of a purplish-grey stone said to be Niedermendig lava from the Rhineland and probably brought in as ballast in a ship trading with the continent. At Aldeby, although the Norman nave walls contain some flint, they consist mainly of an unidentified grey sedimentary rubble stone, some pieces of which are unusually large. As no local source for this stone is known and as its character and the quantity used suggest that it is unlikely to be a locally obtained erratic material from glacial drift, it has probably been imported. The church is barely a mile from the River Waveney.

FLINT AND STONE BANDING

The alliance of stone and knapped flint in alternating bands is a mode of expression in certain flint areas outside East Anglia where suitable stone occurs, like the Wylie valley of Wiltshire and parts of Dorset; but unlike flint and stone chequerwork which is also found in those areas, flint and stone banding is not a strong tradition in East Anglia. There are, however, a few examples from the past, and it has also been used in modern times, as may be seen on the cathedral extensions at Bury St Edmunds and on the south aisle of Boreham church.

The earliest instances of bands of stone within walls of flint are to be found, not surprisingly, in the round towers of early churches. On the eleventh-century tower of Holy Trinity church at Bungay there are stretches of rubble stone laid in the herringbone manner interspersed within its rubble flint fabric. This stone is a light buff colour, probably a sandstone, and is seen as discontinuous lengths about 30 to 45 cm (12 to 18 in) high, at irregular spacings. Although the continuity of this stonework, and consequently its visual impact as banding, has to some extent been impaired by later repairs and alterations, its original purpose would seem to have been decorative rather than structural. At Roughton (21) bands of ferricrete within the flintwork encircle the tower near the base, and on the round tower at Herringfleet, large stones – mainly erratics – form three bands at different levels. Similar features, but less distinct, appear on a few other round towers.

The most important instance of the use of ashlared stone is to be found on the south-west fringe of East Anglia, at Waltham Abbey. There, on the walls of the Abbey's fourteenth-century south chapel (93), bands of knapped flint of differing widths lie between horizontal stripes of ashlared stone, and above the west window two narrow bands of knapped flint and five or six single courses of medieval red brick traverse the stone

22 Alternating bands of knapped flint and stone on the fourteenth-century
      tower of Purleigh church. Note the dipping and tapering of the bands
      at the window arch

gable. Alternating knapped flint and limestone bands also occur on the north vestry at
Surlingham church.

The fourteenth-century church tower walls at Purleigh (22) have alternating bands of
knapped flint and stone, both about 45 cm (18 in) high, which are of particular interest for
the way they meet the pointed arches of the tower windows and west door: as each flint
and stone band nears the curve of the arch, it dips towards the arch focus, tapering to a
voussoir shape in the manner of rusticated coursing around the arches of Renaissance
buildings three or four centuries later. This surely must be unique in Gothic architecture.

On another fourteenth-century Essex tower, at Fingringhoe, there are alternating bands
of stone and knapped flint of roughly similar widths for the full height of the tower (94).
The stone stripes, however, are mostly rendered and, where the rendering has become
detached, the stonework beneath can be seen to be roughly-laid rubble walling stone of an
uncertain type, not ashlar, and so it is likely that the 'stone' stripes were from the outset
intended to be rendered.

At Leiston church, an adventurous design of the nineteenth century by E. B. Lamb, single
courses of squared Crag stone alternate with approximately 90 cm (3 ft) high bands of
flintwork. The character of these walls is enhanced by the originality of their flintwork,
a roughly-coursed mix of flints and non-flint erratics in about equal proportions. All, including the non-flints, are knapped, and this gives the wall an unusual play of textures and
colours from the erratics.

CHAPTER ELEVEN

Triple Composite Flintwork

This category includes all varieties of flintwork in which two other walling materials are allied with any type or types of flint in the same wall. As a complete inventory of all possible permutations of flint with two ancillary materials would be very cumbersome, a limited selection only of some common combinations has been included.

FLINT, LIMESTONE AND ERRATICS

This is one of the most widespread composite combinations and is found in so many Perpendicular churches that it could almost be regarded as a standard technique of later medieval times. The flint may be as-found, knapped or mixed; the stones are often small lumps of freestone, no doubt salvaged from earlier buildings; and the erratics are typically the usual medley of brown and ochre cobbles and boulders.

Claydon church tower is an example where the rubbly flint and erratics are in conventional proportions and the limestone is sparse; by contrast, on the tower walls at Garboldisham and the aisle at New Buckenham, blue-grey knapped flints and small pieces of limestone are laid in a manner similar to that in the walls at Hilborough (91), but with erratics providing intermittent accents of colour.

At Rickinghall Superior church (95), the way that similar materials with rather more erratics have been prepared and ordered has produced walls of a unique and distinctive character. Select knapped flints are dark blue-grey, cleft-faced limestone nodules are creamy-grey, and whole or split non-flint boulder erratics range from dark brown to light buff. The proportion of flint is about equal to the amount of erratics and limestone combined, and all the materials are trimmed to similar sizes and laid in even courses with a little flint galleting, the knapped flints alternating with either limestone or erratic to create a beautifully balanced multi-coloured check in shades of grey, cream and brown.

Limestone batts dressed to the shape of a brick stretcher are prominent features of the well-proportioned mix of flint, limestone and colourful erratics in the coursed walls of the porch of Rattlesden church, where much of the knapped flint and some of the erratics are squared, so that, with the help of a little discreet galleting, no mortar is exposed. With a larger proportion of limestone batts and less telling erratics, similar materials create a pronounced check effect in the coursed aisle and clerestory walls of Great Barton church (96).

FLINT, LIMESTONE AND BRICK

Seen chiefly in churches of the fifteenth century, this mixture at its best has knapped flint, small pieces of smooth limestone and mellow bricks of that particular rich plum red so characteristic of much medieval brick in East Anglia. The bricks mostly show as headers randomly distributed among the stone and flint that make up most of the wall surface; in these proportions, the three materials make a delightfully colourful wall without garishness, and the clerestories of churches at Potter Heigham, Mendham and Ashill (97) provide superb examples. The east wall of Theberton church (98) is similar, but its flints are mainly pebbles instead of the knapped variety; in morning sunlight it is unsurpassed for its richness of colour and texture.

FLINT, BRICK AND ERRATICS

Though not particularly common, this trio is likely to be found almost anywhere in East Anglia. The west end of Coddenham church is an early example of the rougher kind of medieval wall built of flint, erratics and pieces of brick. It is uncoursed and shows a lot of mortar, and its components are of many different sizes. The flints are a random mixture of rubble and cleft or broken pieces; some of the erratics are hackly and others smoothly water-worn, and the brick ingredients are mainly broken pieces that are irregularly placed and for the most part laid out of level.

FLINT, BRICK AND CHALK

Black knapped flint, white rubble nodules, red and buff brick headers or fragments and lumps of white chalk laid in courses, despite their varied shapes, make a lively wall on a nineteenth-century house in Mundford, and the same materials with brick headers set vertically and galleted with chips of broken brick form a colourful boundary wall at Foulden (7). Both these walls exhibit a rustic standard of workmanship typical of work seen in farm buildings and walls in the chalk areas.

FLINT, BRICK AND CARSTONE

Walls of flint, brick and carstone are found mainly in the western part of Norfolk near the carstone sources and are common on vernacular buildings in villages near to and east of Downham Market. In a barn in Wereham (99) undressed lumps of flint and carstone rubble, interspersed with brick headers, are laid roughly coursed, leaving large areas of exposed mortar crudely galleted with carstone. Carstone is the dominant ingredient of these barn walls, but on a cottage in Fincham where the three materials are used in a quite different manner, the visual impact derives from the brick: coursed header bricks, laid on end or nearly so, form irregular long and short sequences between white rubbly flint nodules and intermittent lumps of carstone (100).

FLINT, CARSTONE AND CHALK

This is another mixture likely to be found only in the north-west of Norfolk but even there it is not very common as chalk is not extensively used in building, as we have seen. A cottage group near Fring has walls mainly of roughly-squared blocks of rubble chalk laid in 15 cm (6 in) courses or thereabouts, interspersed with similar-sized carstone blocks and large cleft flints with a few cobbles amongst them. The wide mortar joints are galleted with carstone chips.

FLINT, CARSTONE AND RED ROCK

Only found within a few miles of Hunstanton, this combination is rare except as small patches in rough rubbly walls of very mixed material. One remarkable exception is a section of wall, probably dating from the late sixteenth century, on a farmhouse in Ringstead where fawn-coloured knapped flint, rose-coloured rock and brown carstone make an effective tricolour check pattern (101). The wall is coursed, and within each course the three materials alternate, with occasional variations in their sequence. The relative durability of the materials is well demonstrated by their differential weathering, the flint standing proud of the Red Rock and softer carstone.

CHAPTER TWELVE

Multiple Composite Flintwork

———————————

Multiple mixtures, where flint is one of four or more different materials in a wall, are most likely to be found in places near indigenous stone sources, for example in the carstone and chalk area of west Norfolk or the crag and septaria localities of Suffolk and Essex. Ferricrete appears to be more widely and randomly distributed; it is found mainly in early and medieval churches and seems not to have been much used in later secular buildings.

With four or more materials, there are of course countless possible combinations and within these variety is further increased by the different types of flint. Just a few representative mixtures, therefore, will be described, without differentiating between the flint types.

FLINT, BRICK, LIMESTONE AND ERRATICS

This colourful mix has been found in quite early church walls, for instance the early fourteenth-century south aisle of Kedington church and the south aisle of Coddenham church of a similar date, where the limestone content of the mix is rather sparse. At both these churches the bricks are thin and of irregular sizes; they are a strong bright red and are probably reused Roman material.

FLINT, BRICK, FERRICRETE AND ERRATICS

Apart from its medieval tower and south porch, most of Ardleigh church was designed by William Butterfield, one of the leading exponents of polychrome effects in the architecture of the nineteenth century. It is no surprise, then, that he has delighted here in the diversity of colour available to him from the local materials. Echoing the knapped flint, brick, ferricrete and sundry other stones of the tower fabric, Butterfield disposes smaller pieces of these materials in a random pattern, augmented with knapped erratics to create harmonious walls of great richness (*102*).

FLINT, BRICK, LIMESTONE AND CARSTONE OR FERRICRETE, WITH OR WITHOUT ERRATICS

While mixes containing carstone are mainly local to west Norfolk, those containing ferricrete may be found almost anywhere and the same may be said of mixes containing non-flint erratics. A cottage in Barton Bendish dated 1713 has walls in which rubbly pieces of limestone and carstone are roughly coursed with as-found flints and pale red bricks, and liberally galleted with carstone pebbles. The same materials are also used on later cottages in East Walton but there, buff bricks laid higgledy-piggledy with white flints and less carstone make a softer impression, and in similar mixes on cottages at Boughton ferricrete takes the place of carstone. On the walls of Fincham church, these materials in different proportions, but with roughly knapped black flints and a few erratics, make an entirely different impression.

FLINT, FERRICRETE, SEPTARIA AND CRAG

Sometimes the amount of flint present in a wall may be such a small proportion of the whole as hardly to warrant the mixture being called flintwork, and the east wall of Goldhanger church is an instance where the flint plays only a minor role. It is mainly of rough-coursed dark ferricrete and buff septaria with a few bits of crag. Disposition of such flints as there are, mainly pebbles and cobbles, is irregular, and here and there they are used almost as desultory galleting. Possibly most of them are repair insertions.

FLINT, BRICK, FERRICRETE, CRAG, LIMESTONE, SEPTARIA AND ERRATICS

Blends of these materials, which may include some or all of them in greater or lesser proportions, are found mainly in the south-east of the region. The walls of Ardleigh church tower, for example, are predominantly ferricrete with knapped flint and some brick and crag and a few erratics; Shottisham church walls are an irregular mixture of cobbly flints with bricks and lumps of septaria and crag, and at Salcott the nave walls, mainly of flint and septaria, also contain oddments of limestone and a few large pieces of crag (103). In most of the walls in which these local materials occur, their use is spontaneous and uncontrived. By contrast, on Sir Thomas Lucas's exotic little fishing lodge of 1591 in Bourne Road, Colchester, the walls are a flamboyant mosaic of ferricrete, limestone and septaria spiced with red bricks from the Roman town and liberally galleted with flakes of flint. More colourful even than those walls, the west face of Little Bentley church tower (104) contains all seven of the materials in this selection.

CHAPTER THIRTEEN

Freestone Flushwork

———————————

Flushwork is a style of ornamentation in which ashlared freestone is allied to knapped flint to create architectural patterns and decorative motifs on the external walls of flint buildings. It is the equivalent in masonry of inlaying in cabinetmaking.

Although knapped flint and limestone are combined in flush chequer patterns in other flint areas besides East Anglia, it is only in East Anglia that the contrasting qualities of these two materials inspired a more imaginative and innovative repertoire of designs. This creativity was to blossom into the unique regional art-form now known as flushwork, and was all the more surprising since the stone had to be brought from afar, there being no suitable indigenous freestones. Those used came chiefly from quarries on the Lincolnshire Limestone formation, and were transported most of the way by water.

Given its name because the flint and stone are set flush with each other, flushwork produces a flat wall surface. It is purely surface decoration, and despite the hints of structural meaning suggested by many panelling patterns, the constructional contribution of the stone elements of the system is insignificant because the stone is only a surface treatment applied to a weight-bearing wall. The shallow stone strips used for outlining the patterns were not a structural framework and seem to have been simply mortared onto the rubble-flint backing wall; the spaces they defined were then infilled with knapped flints. In all but inferior work the filling flints were closely fitted and often squared, and, where the patterns required, shaped with immaculate precision. The practice of galleting in flushwork was therefore rarely necessary. A notable exception, however, is the porch at Bunwell where unsquared knapped flint is profusely galleted with flakes of flint packed into the joints.

For many of the smaller and more intricate designs, knapped flints were just mortared into recesses of the required shape that were simply hollowed out of a stone slab background. These hollows are surprisingly shallow, as can be seen, alas, where a flushwork motif has lost its flint infill, like some of those on the clerestory of Coddenham church or the base of Thrandeston church tower. Notwithstanding such losses, it is remarkable, if

23 West elevation of St Ethelbert's Gate,
    Norwich, as drawn by R. Cattermole for
    Britton's *History and Antiquities of the
    See and Cathedral Church of Norwich*,
    published in 1815, prior to restoration

24 Rose window motifs in flushwork in the
    parapet on the west side of St Ethelbert's Gate,
    Norwich, as restored by William Wilkins

we bear in mind the constructional techniques, that so much flushwork has withstood the
ravages of 600 years and more.

It was not long after the re-emergence of knapped flint that flushwork first appeared.
The earliest positively datable example is said to be St Ethelbert's Gate, Norwich, of 1316,
which, although restored by William Wilkins in the nineteenth century, follows the general
composition of the original (23), but with detail differences in the parapet's flushwork
patterns (24). Butley Priory Gatehouse of *c.*1320 is another early example, even if it may
also have been restored. Be that as it may, the quality of the flushwork on both these buildings seems too assured to be the first-fruits of a new art-form, and it is likely therefore that
certain less mature, undated works are earlier.

A precursor of flushwork can be recognized in the late-thirteenth-century octagonal
stage of the round tower of West Somerton church: built of cobbles, it has lancet belfry
openings with stone dressings in the cardinal faces and replicas of these in the diagonals.

25 Flushwork imitation window infilled
    with knapped flint and inset within
    rubble flint walling in the belfry stage
    of the fourteenth-century octagonal
    tower of Old Buckenham church. An
    early example of flushwork: notice the
    stone strip technique in the arch but
    conventional quoining still in the jambs

Although the stone dressings of the replicas are built conventionally like those of the belfry
openings, that is to say, with jamb stones of varied sizes and the arch formed with voussoir
stones, the imitation 'openings' are infilled with squared knapped flints laid completely
flush with the outer face of the stone dressings. Confirmation that these replicas were built
as decoration and are not just blocked, redundant openings is provided internally, where
the sections of wall behind them are seen to be continuous and uninterrupted plain flint
walling without any indications of such blocking.

    Undoubtedly, though, the most convincing archetypes of true flushwork are to be seen
on the octagonal tower of Old Buckenham church (25) and on the octagonal belfry stage
of the round tower at Theberton, where two-light flushwork replicas echo the shape of
the belfry openings, both datable by their Y-tracery as *c.*1300. These must be very early
examples, as they seem to define the moment when flushwork technique was emerging out
of conventional construction, for, whereas the jambs of the dummy windows are still
formed with bonding stones of varied widths in the manner of normal quoins, the arches
are not formed with voussoirs but are shaped from stone strips as in mature flushwork.
The use of knapped flint only in the window shapes, the rest of the wall remaining as
rubble flint, also suggests tentative, early work. Nevertheless, also datable by the inter-
sected tracery of its east window as of about the same period, the flushwork on the chancel
walls at Wiveton (*105*) shows an advance towards maturity both in the confident design of

its stone elements and the fact that the background wall is of knapped flint as well as the infilling of the panels.

Other elementary flushwork can be seen on the towers of Kedington church (*106*) and St Margaret's, Lowestoft: the panels of knapped flint occurring within the rubble flint of the belfry stage at Kedington have already been mentioned, and at Lowestoft, it appears that early flushwork arcading has been interrupted by the insertion of what seem to be later belfry openings.

Ashlared limestone is virtually always used for the stone elements of flushwork. But there are rare exceptions: at Rochford and Canewdon churches, for instance, the very rough-looking unashlared stone in their chequerwork is probably an east coast crag or Kentish Rag from across the Thames estuary; and on the much-repaired fourteenth-century tower of Lawford church the remnants can just be traced of a flushwork panelling pattern in which the knapped flint is enclosed within a framework of dark brown ferricrete.

Many flushwork designs were inspired by familiar architectural features carved from solid stone such as window tracery, cresting and crocketing, etc., and much of their character derives from medieval masons' translations of those three-dimensional features into flat patterns. The early imitation windows in the octagonal belfries at Old Buckenham and Theberton are facsimiles in flushwork of complete architectural features, but the same concept was also applied to smaller motifs. This is well demonstrated on the porch of Pulham St Mary church (26), where the openwork quatrefoil cresting of the parapet is simulated in flushwork within the panelling of the side walls, and on the porches at Southwold (*107*) and Ufford, stone relief carving in the front parapets is interpreted as flushwork in the side parapets.

Although a few secular works have flushwork decoration, it is mostly to be found on churches. East Anglia has over 450 churches with flushwork on some part of their structure: more than ninety per cent of these lie to the east of a dog-leg line from Cromer to Newmarket to Colchester, the rest being more widely scattered, mainly in Essex, west Norfolk and Cambridgeshire. The most surprising is in March, in the Fens and some distance from flint country, where the upper parts of the clerestory walls of an otherwise stone church are faced with knapped flint, and flint flushwork emblems occur between the clerestory windows.

Within the whole range of freestone flushwork compositions, certain themes can be identified which form the basis of virtually all designs in the medium, and each is typified by particular features. While many compositions are based on a single theme, others often embrace elements of more than one. The major themes are *Inset*, *Chequer*, *Emblems*, *Tracery and Panelling*, and *Serial Flushwork*. These are individually described below.

INSET

In its fully mature manifestation, flushwork is a patterning system which completely fills the wall areas to which it is applied, these usually being defined by the architectural

26 Open quatrefoil parapet
motif interpreted in
flushwork within the
upper stage panelling
on the side walls of the
porch at Pulham St Mary
church

features of the building. But there are some instances where flushwork features or stone motifs are isolated within a flint background, and do not form part of an overall design. Some of these date from the Decorated Period of the fourteenth century, while others are from the late fifteenth, and so the concept should not be seen simply as an elementary stage in the development of the art of flushwork.

Replica windows are characteristic early motifs in this manner; simple window shapes of freestone set flush with the wall face are typical, like those echoing the Y-tracery of the belfry openings in the towers of Old Buckenham and Theberton. From the later fourteenth century, the knapped flint octagonal belfry that crowns the round tower of Potter Heigham church also has sham windows of mature flushwork in alternate faces of the octagon. They

27 'Norwich' style flushwork in the fifteenth-century parapet of St Clement's church tower,
   Norwich, in which the knapped-flint merlon and indent zones are separated by stone strips
   and contain inset relief stone lozenge motifs

are faithful representations in flat stone of the belfry openings, which have cusped tracery,
and are surmounted by raised stone hoodmoulds with sculptured label-stops, all of them
identical to the corresponding features of the belfry openings. The imitation window, in
both as-found and knapped backgrounds, is a feature of several other octagonal belfry
stages of round towers, whether they are an addition to an earlier tower (Bedingham) or
contemporary with the circular stage (Thorpe Abbotts). The flushwork window theme also
appears in Perpendicular three-light form at one end of the brick-diapered clerestory of
Great Witchingham church.

Single, isolated flush motifs within a broad field of knapped flint are well shown in two
contrasting medieval examples that are separated in time by about one-and-a-half centuries. At Wickmere (40), the earlier, a small equal-limbed cross botoné is set in the plain
white knapped flint of the clerestory wall between each window, and on the massive tower
of Lavenham church five-pointed stars of stone stand isolated within a dark knapped-flint
background.

The porch of St Andrew's, Barton Bendish (108), also has individual stone motifs –
blank shields, saltire crosses and five panels with shallow relief carving that are set within
the knapped flint of the front wall and, just above the plinth of the rubble and brick side
walls, a row of blank shields with knapped flint between them. The inset motifs of the
front wall represent a departure from the conventional subjects found on the majority of
contemporary flushwork porches.

Inset motifs are the basis of an unusual style of flushwork that appears on the parapets
of several church towers in Norwich (27) and a few others elsewhere in Norfolk, namely

28 Flushwork motifs inset within coursed flint cobbles on the tower parapet of Benacre church

Blofield, Burgh next Aylsham, Coltishall, Ditchingham, Griston, Northrepps and West-wick. On these parapets, the knapped flint surface is simply divided by plain stone strips into zones that correspond with the parapet crenellations, and stone motifs are inset within these zones. They are generally flush with the flint but some are carved in shallow relief. Blank shields and lozenge shapes are typical motifs for the insets of this 'Norwich' style, although at Griston the main motifs are crossed keys and crossed swords.

The fourteenth-century tower of Benacre church is largely built of variably-coursed cobble flints, but the parapet walls are evenly coursed with cobbles that are laid upright. On the evidence of its better condition and its oddly-laid cobbles, the parapet has probably been restored, making it difficult to attribute a confident date to its simple but unusual flushwork (28). This consists of separate emblems, about 1 m (3.4 ft) square, inset into the background: the naivety of this design certainly suggests early work, and so if it is a res-toration, original details may well have been reset.

CHEQUER

Chequer flushwork is generally thought of as a chessboard pattern of alternating flint and stone squares, but there are also rectangular versions, as on Thompson church tower plinth, and occasionally triangles, as at Norwich Guildhall and Elveden church. The stone components are ashlared freestone cut to true shape and laid with corners touching, and the flints are knapped and usually, though not always, squared.

The size of the grid in most chessboard patterns is about 15 to 23 cm (6 to 9 in) square, even if sometimes the squares are smaller, as in some of the decoration on Walberswick church, and occasionally larger, as on the parapets of Horringer church. They may be straight or diagonal (when diagonal, the pattern is sometimes called lozenge), and chequer patterns of both kinds appear on the plinths and parapets of many church towers and the walls of several church porches, e.g. Southwold (*107*) and Woolpit with level squares, Walsham le Willows (*109*) with diagonal squares, and Stowlangtoft (*110*) which has both types. At the latter two places the church wall plinths are also extensively chequered. Sometimes the pattern covers a whole wall area, as on two well-known Norfolk buildings: King's Lynn's fifteenth-century Guildhall with its Elizabethan extension and adjacent Victorian Town Hall is patterned with level squares, and the east wall of Norwich Guildhall of 1535 has diagonal squares, with triangles in the gable.

As chequerwork is essentially a decoration of tonal contrasts, black flints are generally used to offset the lighter hues of the stonework. Where cortication has faded the flints, as on the porch of the Prior's Lodging at Castle Acre, the intensity of contrast between the two materials has been diminished naturally, but deliberate tonal restraint in chequerwork designs is rare. It is, however, beautifully done in the upper parts of the east wall of Burnham Thorpe church (*111*), where squares of white flint merge in quiet harmony with the warm grey stone. There can be little doubt that this light flintwork is the result of considered selection rather than fortuitous cortication because in the chequerwork of the lower part of the wall all the flints are evenly dark, quite obviously by selection. In this darker work the chequering differs from the chessboard style of the white flint: the dado has rectangular chequer and above this the pattern is more irregular with panels of different sizes and proportions.

A variation on the chequer theme which could be called a lapped chequer is a type where the stone elements are a little wider than the flint panels so that they slightly overlap each other in consecutive courses, thus suggesting they have a weight-bearing role rather than being purely a veneer. The tower of St Mary's, Luton (*112*) is an impressive example. The style is not, however, typical to East Anglia; it is more characteristic of the local vernacular in parts of Wiltshire where both flint and stone are indigenous.

Although the chessboard pattern is manifestly an important part of the flushwork tradition and, like all flushwork designs, an expression of specialized local craftsmanship, it is not a typical decorative theme of mainstream Gothic ornament outside the flushwork idiom. Its rectilinear discipline might perhaps be regarded as more in character with the formality of classical architecture, but there are hardly any instances of such association. One interesting example, though, is the tower of Hopton church where an eighteenth-century belfry stage rests uneasily on a medieval substructure (*29*). It is a simple design with classical architectural elements in walls faced entirely in chessboard chequer.

29 Hopton church tower. Chequer flushwork on the classical belfry stage,
built on the medieval lower stage after the fall of the original belfry in
the early eighteenth century

30 Flushwork emblems on the base of the fifteenth-century tower of Woodbridge church. *Left*, a stone motif in a flint background. *Right*, flint motifs within a stone framework

EMBLEMS

This term embraces the countless small flushwork devices that occur as individual displays or as elements of larger compositions. They may be deployed singly, or as repeated or varied features in a decorative band giving emphasis to particular architectural elements, or they may be incorporated as focal points within extensive overall patterning.

In their most usual manifestation, emblem designs take the form of freestone panels, typically about 1 m (3.4 ft) square more or less, into which knapped flint shapes are fitted to express a wide repertoire of ideas.

Foremost amongst the subject matter for emblems is Gothic tracery, a purely non-representational theme. Key motifs include the ubiquitous trefoils and quatrefoils with rounded or pointed lobes, soufflets, daggers and mouchettes. Other foliated shapes that derive from tracery play supporting roles, and are artfully adapted to fill the awkward corners of all manner of compositions. Certain ideas constantly recur: a quatrefoil in a circle that is eccentrically placed within an outer circle below a pair of tadpole-like mouchettes (30), and three or more curved mouchettes within a circle that, when seen from a distance, create the effect of a wheel with curved spokes, are favourite devices.

Another emblem theme comprises representational motifs. In addition to their decorative function, they convey religious, symbolic and commemorative meanings. Sacred

31 Geometric emblems on the base of the tower of Hawstead church. The central figure appears
to be derived from trefoiled window-heads, two with rounded lobes and two with pointed

monograms, crowned initials and heraldic devices are typical subjects. Rarer designs include lilies in a vase, as in the clerestory of Grundisburgh church, crowned swords, as on
the porch buttresses at Great Cressingham, crossed keys, as on Kelsale porch, and crossed
keys and crossed swords, as in the tower parapet of Griston church.

Non-figurative designs comprise a third emblem theme. Owing little to Gothic tracery,
stylized foliage forms and the geometry of circles, lines and triangles are used to create
abstract designs in flint and stone. There are some striking examples on the church tower
at Hawstead (31), all of which show fine workmanship in the fitting of flint to stone; others
in the clerestory of Cotton church have distinctive foliage and abstract motifs not found
elsewhere.

The subjects of these designs may be depicted either in knapped flint within a framework
of stone, like the quatrefoil and other figures in the right-hand panel in the illustration
from the plinth of Woodbridge church tower (30), or in freestone against a background of
dark knapped flint like the crowned initial M in the left-hand panel. In general, it seems
that tracery-based motifs appear as knapped flint in stone backgrounds, whereas representational features are usually depicted in stone on a flint background. Geometrical
abstractions can often be read as stone on flint or vice versa. Sometimes the motif itself is
composed of the two materials together, as happens in the small crosses formed in stone
and flint on the stone faces of the porch buttresses of Dickleburgh church.

East Anglian churches have countless examples of emblem ornament of all kinds on
various parts of the buildings. Some of the finest include the tower parapets at Horham

32 Superb crowned initials and monograms in flushwork over the entrance arch of
Rickinghall Superior church porch

and Rougham (39), where two lily-in-a-vase motifs are superimposed on perhaps the
largest flushwork crowned M to be found anywhere; the superb nave parapet at Rattlesden
with its sixteen different emblems; the clerestories at Cotton and Walsham le Willows
(109); the porches at Woodbridge, Ufford and Rickinghall Superior (32); and the buttresses
at Northwold, Elmswell and Theberton and on the seventeenth-century tower of Dalham.

TRACERY AND PANELLING

Window tracery themes in flushwork are derived directly from contemporary styles of
stone window tracery. Typically they appear on the octagonal belfries of certain round
towers where they mimic the tracery of the belfry openings, but they also sometimes occur
as wall decoration, either as single window likenesses, as on Butley Priory Gatehouse and
the dramatic remnant of the fourteenth-century priory church at Little Walsingham (113),
or as repeated features in a larger pattern like the blank arcading on Worstead church
tower. The supreme example of flushwork window-tracery patterns displayed on the grand
scale is at the church of St Michael at Coslany, Norwich (114), where flushwork interpret-
ations of the window designs cover the fifteenth-century south aisle and the restored
chancel walls. Apart from its exquisite craftsmanship, the characteristic which makes this
stand out as work of special quality is the subtle variation in the widths of the stone
elements of the design. The flushwork tracery patterns (two, three and four panels wide)
have primary frameworks in stone strips of normal width; the ogee arches of the midway
tracery are slightly narrower; the head tracery elements are yet more slender; and the
smaller details finer still. The knapped flint to fit this intricate stonework is shaped with an
apt precision.

Another tracery pattern, the rose window in flushwork, is more of a rarity. St Ethelbert's
Gate, Norwich, has one in its east gable and three on its west parapet (23, 24); although
the three are not the original designs, the pattern of the east-facing one, even if restored,
seems to be authentic. Flushwork rose-window replicas also appear in each face of the
distinctive parapet of the Perpendicular tower of Deopham church (115).

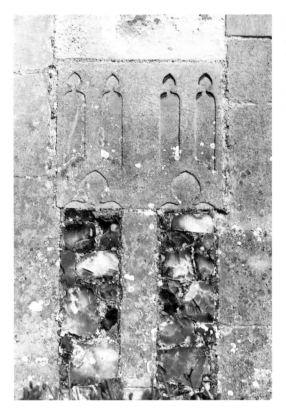

33 Shallow-sunk foliations in stone heads
of flushwork flint panels on the porch
of Thornham Magna church

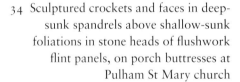

34 Sculptured crockets and faces in deep-
sunk spandrels above shallow-sunk
foliations in stone heads of flushwork
flint panels, on porch buttresses at
Pulham St Mary church

Panelling in flushwork, which is inherently expressive of the Perpendicular architectural style, lies at the heart of the mature East Anglian flushwork tradition and is the basis of many of the outstanding works in the medium. Its definitive features are vertically-proportioned panels of knapped flint framed by ashlar stone, singly or in sequences. In their simplest form, the panels are rectangular and bounded by plain vertical and horizontal strips of stone, as on the porch at Market Weston church. In a few such instances, shallow sinkings barely 5 mm (0.2 in) deep in the stonework above the panels convey tenuous impressions of foliated tracery, and though some of them are just cheap repairs to proper flushwork, most seem to be of original construction, as on the church porches at

35 Flushwork panelling on the Victorian chancel east wall of Cromer church

Finningham and Thornham Magna (33). A delightful refinement of the concept occurs on the porch buttresses at Pulham St Mary church where the spandrels above the shallow stone foliations are deeply sunk, allowing space for crockets and small sculptured faces in full relief (34). In most flushwork panelling, though, the tops of the flint panels are of traceried arch shapes with corresponding foliated stonework. Sometimes secondary motifs are introduced below the upper tracery (35), or two panels may be paired beneath a single traceried head terminating with a crocketed finial (119). Within the panels, the knapped flints may be squared or unshaped, and where they conform to curved or pointed backgrounds, they are usually trimmed with unerring accuracy.

Whereas flushwork panelling is frequently used to adorn the buttresses, parapets, plinths and dado friezes (35) of churches, it is displayed to its most spectacular effect where it covers extensive areas of wall, as on the Gatehouse of St Osyth's Priory. Although there are few secular buildings with flushwork to equal the luxuriance of that found on churches, this sumptuous work built in the late fifteenth century to provide private rooms for the prior, can rival any church in the splendour of its flushwork decoration. The south front (116), from foliated plinth to chequered battlements, is entirely patterned with narrow panelling that is skilfully designed to accord with the architectural features of the façade. Bisected by a string course into two stages, the façade's lower stage is panelled in three bands, with short panels in the bottom band and taller ones in the upper two. Above the string course there are two bands of panelling – short lower panels and the upper ones almost three times their height, with superb traceried and crocketed paired heads and crocketed finials between.

The fifteenth-century Gatehouse of St John's Abbey in Colchester, much restored in the

36 Alternating zones of single- and double-width flushwork panelling on
the west front of the fifteenth-century tower of Eye church

37 Flushwork panelling and emblems around the west doorway of the tower
of Coltishall church

nineteenth century, has flushwork comparable to St Osyth's, but the overall design of the
panelling is less well related to the architectural features of the building.

It is on the towers, clerestories and porches of certain East Anglian churches that the
greatest accomplishments in flushwork panelling are to be seen. Three church towers in
particular, Redenhall, Eye (36) and Laxfield, stand out from all others for the extent and
splendour of their flushwork panelling. The towers themselves are of an imposing design,
with four stages and polygonal buttresses, and they are so close architecturally as to suggest the hand of the same master mason in all three; only in the openings of the top stages
do significant differences appear in the west fronts. The concept of the flushwork is also the
same on them all. It covers the whole of the west front and comprises panelling bands of
different heights, the panels in successive bands often being half the width of those above
or below. The panels in general have simple foliated heads and the main visual impact
of the composition is the interplay of the single and double-width panels. Besides these
three towers, only a few others have notable flushwork on their main stages: these include
St Lawrence's, Ipswich (117), Southwold (118) and Worstead. About twenty others have
panelling, chequer or emblems around their west doorways, as at Coltishall (37).

About 250 church towers in East Anglia have parapets decorated with flushwork.
Many of these have the typical arrangement of panelling in the merlons, and emblems or
panelling below the indents, but by no means all follow this pattern. Single-stage parapet
designs of greater originality and intricacy are seen at Kersey (38) and Ringland amongst
others, while of the two-stage parapets with well-proportioned panelling Great Barton and
Rougham (39) must count amongst the finest.

38 Finialled quatrefoils within cinquefoil panels in flushwork on the fine single-stage tower parapet of Kersey church

39 The two-stage tower parapet of Rougham church, with fine tracery-based serial flushwork in the frieze, and panelling and emblems in the stepped top stage. Note the large crowned M with two superimposed lily-in-a-vase motifs

40 Simple flushwork panels in the sixteenth-century clerestory of Bressingham church

41 Elaborate display of different flushwork themes in the clerestory of Woolpit church. Probably fifteenth century

Panelling is the basis of many clerestory flushwork patterns, austere or embellished. One of the sparsest designs appears on the low windowless clerestory of Tunstead church, which has just a single band of blank arcading with quatrefoils in the arcade spandrels. By contrast, in the mature design at Cavendish, the walls between each lofty transomed three-light window are patterned with four slender panels in two stages, the lower panel heads being aligned with the window transoms and the upper panels united in pairs under a common traceried and crocketed head at the level of the window tracery.

Closely related architecturally to the Cavendish design, the clerestory of Long Melford's splendid church less than four miles away has almost identical three-light transomed windows, a similar parapet and similar flushwork panelling; but because of the closer spacing of the windows due to the clerestory having twice as many windows as there are arches in the nave arcade below, there is only sufficient width of wall between them for two panels. As at Cavendish, the two panels are united under a traceried and crocketed head. Panelling of the same pattern is repeated on the walls of the Lady Chapel, which is entirely faced with flushwork. Strangely, however, on the three gables of the east wall, the discipline of the rhythmic panelling completely breaks down: each gable displays a large stone square surrounded by an oddly indiscriminate selection of unrelated flushwork motifs. Nevertheless, despite this aberration, Long Melford church surely stands as one of the great manifestations of the glory of flushwork.

The most telling clerestory designs are often those with uncomplicated panelling patterns whose simple rhythms, echoing the regularity of the fenestration, seem to harmonize more naturally with a sequence of clerestory windows than individual emblems or chequerwork do. This is well illustrated by a comparison of the designs at Bressingham (40) and Woolpit (41). The clerestories of these two churches are similar architecturally, but their flushwork could hardly be more different: restrained elegance at Bressingham and extravagant virtuosity at Woolpit.

New porches were added to many churches during the prosperous fifteenth and sixteenth centuries and they were frequently decorated lavishly with stone carving and flushwork, particularly on their front walls. They show a fascinating variety of flushwork detail, though they differ little in general architectural design. Most of them rely on panelling as the basis for the flushwork composition, which is often augmented with other themes; but it is the conviction with which this decoration relates to a porch's architectural features that differentiates the best from the ordinary. The well-integrated panelling on the porches at Hitcham (42) or Ufford, amongst others, demonstrates a conscious affinity between architecture and ornament, whereas on Ixworth porch the flushwork appears awkward and ill-considered, particularly the band of panels over the entrance which bears no relationship to the shape of the wall it occupies (43).

A few porches have flushwork on their side walls as well as on the front. Among the most sumptuous are those at Woodbridge, Preston St Mary (44), Pulham St Mary, Glemsford (119) and Chelmsford Cathedral (front cover). The last is two-storied and is remarkable for the variety of ideas in the lavish flushwork of its side walls: single panels in the plinth and parapet, diagonal chequer in the lower stage, and paired panels below

42 Flushwork on Hitcham church porch, well related to the porch architecture

43 Ixworth church porch. Here, the flushwork does not integrate well with the architecture of the porch

finialled and crocketed heads, surmounted by a row of emblems, in the upper stage. Between the emblems there are square panels of rich red brickwork which incorporate blue-brick lozenge motifs. This inclusion of decorative brickwork within a flint and stone flushwork composition is unique.

Flushwork panelling of an entirely different kind, in association with an extraordinary window, in the east wall of Barsham church (120) makes a singular contribution to the East Anglian flushwork genre. Its materials are the same as in conventional flushwork but the difference lies in the fact that the stone strips are laid over the whole wall area in a diagonal lattice formation, creating a continuous pattern of diamonds, and where the stone diagonals meet the edges of the pointed-arched east window, their lines are continued across it as a grid of diagonal mullions, so that the pattern of diamonds remains unbroken over the whole elevation from the ground to the apex of the gable. The original date of this unorthodox spectacle is uncertain, but its uniqueness and the similarity of the lattice pattern to the Etchingham shield are so striking that there must surely be a connection. Indeed, the shape of the window is that of a shield upside down! Robert Hume, chaplain to the patron, Sir Edward Etchingham, was rector from 1533 to 1554, and he or his successor could have been responsible for the east-end design. Thus, a sixteenth-century date seems a probability. The stonework of the window had to be extensively restored after heavy damage from a lightning strike in 1906.

44 Flushwork panelling on the front and side walls of the fifteenth-century north porch of Preston St Mary church

SERIAL FLUSHWORK

Serial flushwork is a type of continuous or repetitive decoration that is sometimes applied on the horizontal elements of a building and may consist of recurrent motifs or sinuous linear features. The former are well shown above the windows in the parapet of the church of St Michael at Coslany (*114*). Both kinds appear on Coddenham church where, between the merlons of the south aisle parapet, ribbons of simple repetitive cresting alternate with sequences of replicated foliations, and in the north clerestory parapet, whose flint infilling is now regrettably lost, there are twining plant forms and wavy tracery. Wavy flushwork, with the flintwork still in place, can be seen weaving between the emblems in the parapet frieze on Rougham tower (*39*) and in the side parapets of Ufford church porch, where it echoes the relief stone carving of the front gable.

Lettering in flushwork is another form of running ornament and it is undeniable that inscriptions shaped in stone within a dark flint setting make effective decoration, irrespective of the meaning they convey. Over the entrance arches of the porches at East Tuddenham (*45*) and Swannington churches there are examples in Lombardic characters, and on the tower of Southwold church letters in the same script are individually crowned and follow the curvature of the arch over the great west window (*118*). Gothic script in short lengths of text occurs on church tower parapets at Rougham (*39*) and Badwell Ash. But there is no finer Gothic calligraphy in flushwork than the inscription which extends for the full length of the plinth on the north aisle of Stratford St Mary church (*46*).

45 Flushwork inscription in Lombardic script on East Tuddenham church porch

46 The inscription on the fifteenth-century plinth on the north aisle of Stratford St Mary church
    shows the effectiveness of Gothic script as linear flushwork decoration

CHAPTER FOURTEEN

Flushwork Derivatives

BRICK FLUSHWORK

This is a flush decorative wall patterning in which a framework of brick defines the pattern and encloses knapped flint. Otherwise it is similar to freestone flushwork. As brick is less amenable than stone to being formed into complex shapes, brick flushwork cannot match the intricacies found in stonework and is consequently limited to simple designs without much elaboration. Brick flushwork is quite a rarity and most examples of it are from the late Perpendicular period or later.

In the octagonal belfries of Old Catton church tower and the orphaned tower of St Benedict's, Norwich, which lost its parent church in an air raid in 1942, flushwork imitation windows are formed with bricks instead of the more usual limestone. At St Benedict's, apparently a fourteenth-century round tower with a contemporary octagonal belfry, the brick flushwork on the belfry in the form Y-tracery (*121*) is probably the earliest known example of this kind of work and seems scarcely later than the earliest freestone flushwork.

Brick flushwork is occasionally seen in later restorations of church tower parapets. There is simple late-medieval panelling at Caistor St Edmund (*122*), and the medieval tower of Ringsfield church has a seventeenth-century brick parapet (*123*) with two-stage flushwork panelling in which the upper and lower panels are staggered in relation to each other in a manner reminiscent of diaper work. Simpler panelling from Victorian times crowns the round tower at Roughton (*21*) and the stepped parapet of Ardleigh's square tower.

The flint porch at Great Barton church has a plinth only of brick flushwork panelling, and on a small vestry on the north side of Gosbeck church, rebuilt in the 1840s, black knapped flint walls with brick quoins have a stepped parapet with simple rectangular panels of brick flushwork decoration.

A few brick porches of the fifteenth and sixteenth centuries also have flushwork. At Great Bealings, a blank arcade of narrow knapped flint panels that are no wider than the brick headers separating them, forms the plinth of the north porch, and similar panels separated by bricks-on-end decorate the porch parapet and buttresses at Ixworth Thorpe church. The best brick flushwork is to be found on the porch at Great Ashfield (*124*) where some of the brick panel heads are shaped and perforated to receive the knapped flint infilling.

An unusual kind of knapped flint decoration, possibly definable as flushwork, although it is rather different from mainstream styles, occurs on the porch of East Winch church. In its brick gable, inserts of knapped flint echo the indented shapes of the flint infilling between the block-bonded brickwork dressings on the jambs of the porch archway. Similarly derived shapes in knapped flint can also be seen as decorative inserts within ferricrete and rubble flint on the stair turret of Lawford church tower.

The diaper-like panelling at Ringsfield (*123*), the diaper clerestory at Great Witchingham (*71*) and the brick chequers at Weybourne (*58*), Saxlingham and New Buckenham (*59*) pose the question as to where a distinction can be drawn between diaper and chequer on the one hand and brick flushwork on the other. As there is no precise demarcation between these classifications, their differentiation might perhaps be based on a conjecture as to the designer's aesthetic intent. Was a particular composition intended to be simply a pattern in flint and brick, or was it envisaged as an interpretation in these materials of conventional freestone flushwork?

PROUDWORK

As mentioned above, proudwork is a system of wall enrichment in which moulded free-stone members are set proud of the wall face, thus framing or enclosing panels of knapped flint. By comparison with flushwork where flint and stone contribute equally to the decorative impact, in proudwork the stone assumes visual dominance and the flint becomes just the background material of the wall. The two techniques can be directly compared in the north clerestory of Wymondham Abbey, where the two eastern bays are panelled with proudwork while the seven western bays are in flushwork.

The earliest uses of both flushwork and proudwork seem to have occurred at about the same time – in the early fourteenth century, but at widely separated localities. Butley Priory Gatehouse is said to have the earliest datable flushwork though there is no certainty that what is seen today is not part of later restoration work. With little doubt, the earliest proudwork may be assumed to include that on the early-fourteenth-century aisle walls of Bottisham church, where the spandrels above moulded blank arches of stone are infilled with knapped flint, and, from a little later, the simulated windows in the restored front and rear walls of Burnham Norton Friary Gatehouse, if they faithfully represent the original. It is therefore at least as likely as not that proudwork appeared before flushwork. Certainly the infilling of recessed wall areas seems a more likely initial realization of the decorative possibilties of flint knapping than a radical innovation such as flushwork.

47 Proudwork on the nave buttresses
of Lowestoft church

Whichever may have been the earlier development, proudwork never became established as a universal idiom like flushwork, probably because of its greater cost and the burgeoning enthusiasm throughout the region for the new flushwork art-form. Proudwork is not very common, and there are perhaps about fifty buildings, mostly churches, on which it occurs. It is usually applied only to relatively small areas, generally taking the form of panelling, such as on buttresses at Lowestoft (47) and Great Massingham churches, on plinths at Weasenham St Peter, Woodbridge, Blakeney and Happisburgh, and on a few church tower parapets like those at St Gregory's, Norwich, Castle Acre (48), and the neighbouring churches at Mattishall (*125*), North Tuddenham and Shipdham.

Imitation windows in proudwork appear in the octagonal stages of four round towers, Bylaugh, Poringland, Quidenham and Stanford. Proudwork panels simulating three-light transomed windows with straight heads are uncomfortably interposed in the clerestory fenestration of Northwold church, and a sham bay window on a small annex of *c.*1500 on the north side of Gipping church disguises a fireplace within.

A particularly interesting application is that on the front wall and buttresses of Southwold church porch, where some of the recessed flint panels between the raised and moulded stonework incorporate flush stone features. Thus, the complementary art-forms of flushwork and proudwork are combined within a single work.

48 Proudwork on the
single-stage parapet
and angle buttresses of
Castle Acre church tower

RELIEF FLUSHWORK

This self-contradictory description applies to an uncommon kind of decoration similar to true flushwork except that the flintwork infill between the freestone members is of an un-knapped variety such as rubble or cobbles. However skilfully such flints are laid, a flat surface over stone and flint cannot be achieved in the manner of true flushwork and the textural contrast between the two materials is inevitably more apparent.

The plinth decoration of Horham church tower (*126*) is a medieval example where rubble flintwork of quite contorted shapes, partly as-found and partly cleft, forms the infill of foliated panels. However, in view of the high quality of the flushwork on the rest of the tower, this may be just a cheap replacement of original knapped work that had deteriorated.

Simple panelling is also the decorative theme on the parapet of Sudbourne church tower (*127*). Slender trefoiled panels in the merlons and wider cinquefoiled ones below the indents are filled with flint cobbles in hues of yellow and brown which harmonize closely with the warm buff stonework of the panelling framework. The gable of Salcott church porch has a comparable surface texture and tonal blend but there the panel infillings within the limestone framework are rubble, cobble and knapped flints mixed with septaria. Both these works are probably nineteenth-century restorations.

Non-flint cobble erratics with occasional rubble and split flints are the principal ingredients in the non-stone squares of a chequer pattern which covers virtually the whole of the nineteenth-century church at Papworth St Agnes (*128*). Like St Mary's, Luton (*112*), the pattern is a lapped chequer and it is perhaps open to question whether it qualifies at all for consideration as flushwork – true or relief. Are the stone squares just a veneer as in traditional flushwork, or are they blocks of structural masonry? This poses another question: is flushwork necessarily only a veneer technique, or does it embrace any flush pattern of flint with stone or brick?

CHAPTER FIFTEEN

Walls of Varied Flintwork

————————————

No review of East Anglia's flint architecture would be complete without mention of the sometimes sudden and sometimes subtle variations in the character or style of flintwork within a wall and the abrupt changes in building material that are so often seen on many medieval flint churches.

Church towers in particular frequently show variations in workmanship or material within their height, and these do not always occur at stage levels, nor do they necessarily represent different phases of building or rebuilding. There seem to be no definite explanations for such variations and the reasons for them may well be different in different cases. One simple theory is that the materials came from an alternative source. Another possibility is that they represent stages in the work when there was a change of mason actually laying the flints, it being most unlikely that any two craftsmen would achieve the same balance of ingredients, particularly when the building material is a random mixture.

Notable among eleventh-century round church towers that show marked changes of material in their walls are those at Bessingham (3), Gayton Thorpe and Roughton (21). At Bessingham, ferricrete is used for the first 3 m (10 ft), then single courses of flints and ferricrete are followed by a three-metre section of rubble flint, above which the walling material reverts to ferricrete, with flintwork being used for the later parapet. At Gayton Thorpe, the bottom 2 m (6.5 ft) is built mainly with blocks of carstone and silver carr, above which the rest of the wall is rubble flint, but a marked change in the character of the flintwork occurs in the top few feet below the belfry string course. On the Roughton tower, a change from flint to ferricrete as the main walling material occurs just below the belfry openings.

On the later round towers of Edingthorpe and Potter Heigham, whose main fabric is coursed cobbles, there are drifts of knapped flints at irregular intervals which seem to bear little relationship to any decorative scheme. As they are extensive and integrate well with the general walling, they are unlikely to be areas of repair work, and so would appear to be part of the original construction. Random flintwork variations that are infinitely more chaotic are to be seen on the south wall of the square tower at Kedington in work that appears to be a re-casing of the tower's lower stage.

By contrast with these arbitrary variations, a subtle change in the proportions of the wall's ingredients occurs about halfway up on the early-fourteenth-century unbuttressed tower of Thurne church: the lower part is mainly cobbles with a significant quantity of knapped flints, some quite large, but in the upper part, an increase in the rubble flint content and a deficiency in knapped components alters the overall texture. Surprisingly, though, this is not particularly noticeable because the change occurs gradually and the overall colour balance of the cobbles, rubble and knapped flints used in the wall hardly varies.

A more deliberate and capricious transition in the character of the walling between ground and parapet is perpetrated on the west front of the church tower at Little Bentley. At the level of the west door in the lower stage, the wall is a colourful balance of black knapped flint, red brick headers, squared pieces of crag and limestone, nodules of septaria, occasional lumps of ferricrete and cobbly erratics, seven different materials in all (*104*). Above this, the crag, limestone, septaria and ferricrete diminish and brick increases almost to the extent of forming an open chequer, but it soon fades to yield dominance to the flint. On most of the second stage, flint still dominates but there is some brick; near the top of this stage and in the whole of the upper one, the appearance alters dramatically as a result of the introduction of small lumps of dark ferricrete (or carstone) and whiter flints that together produce a contrasty, speckled effect. The parapet reverts to the comparative calm of black and white flint, although still speckly.

A fascinating feat of building artistry is achieved on the nave of Gipping church where the composition of the wall, both in the arrangement and proportions of its materials, gradually changes within its height. The lower parts are a roughly-coursed random mix of flint, limestone and brown erratics; then higher up, the erratics progressively diminish and eventually disappear while the coursing becomes more regular and the spacing of the flint and limestone less random, until at the top of the wall they form a clear chequer pattern. This premeditated artifice, the gradual change in a pattern's emphasis within the height of a wall, is also used on the north side of Great Barton church (*96*), the effect there being achieved by a progressive increase in the size of the limestone batts.

Changes in walling style often occur when later building is added to an existing structure. Blundeston church offers two instances of this: the Norman round tower, which is built of coursed rubble flint, has been heightened by the addition of an Early English belfry, and the walls of this stage, while maintaining the same coursing and scale of material as the Norman work, introduce red bricks into the fabric. As similar bricks have also been used for blocking the redundant Norman belfry openings below and in other repairs, the transition is not too obvious and the addition almost appears to be part of the original structure. When, at the same time, the nave was widened on the south side, the additional height required for the nave west wall was also built in a mixture of flint and brick, unlike the plain flintwork of the original part of the wall.

Abrupt changes of material are often seen on round towers where octagonal belfry stages were added during the fourteenth and fifteenth centuries. In contrast to the rubble flint of the circular stages, the walls of these belfries were sometimes faced with knapped flint, as for example at Rickinghall Inferior, or patterned with bricks, as at Needham.

Likewise, when the major rebuilding of a nave or chancel or the aisle walls was undertaken in later medieval times, the lower part of an earlier rubble flint wall was often retained as a base for new work built in a quite different style of flintwork – usually separated by a cill or string course. This is very evident at East Walton church where, below the window cills, nave walls of probable Norman origin are a rough mix of flint rubble and carstone, but above, where they were rebuilt in the fifteenth century, they are of select-knapped flint. Abrupt changes of this kind also occur on the chancel walls of Great Ellingham church, but in this instance, as the whole wall was probably built at the same time, the different treatment given to each of its three stages seems to be part of a predetermined scheme of decoration: below the window cills the wall is uncoursed rubble flint; at the level of the windows it is faced with rough-squared knapped flint; and in the top stage the two styles of flintwork used in the lower stages reappear in the alternating squares of a chequer pattern (49).

Some of these flintwork changes within a building's walls can be seen to be deliberate, whereas others are clearly not the result of predetermined design and seem to have arisen from circumstances at which we can now only guess. Nevertheless, both are part of the constructional history of the building in which they occur, and time and familiarity have often mellowed their incongruity.

Regrettably, variations of another sort are all too common, namely the scars of unsympathetic repairs that time cannot heal. Areas of unsuitable pointing, alien flints, uncoursed insertions in coursed work, strident patches of brick and many other inept and cheap repairs and blockings of redundant openings mar the faces of flint walls of all periods.

Ancient walls are of course bound to need maintenance from time to time, but when flints are falling out and have to be reset, or when the mortar jointing has weathered or deteriorated to the extent that repointing is required, the necessary repairs should not be so harsh as to change a wall's appearance so much that its essential character is impaired. Although ordinary walls of as-found and mixed materials, whether coursed or uncoursed, will unquestionably look different after repointing, their character can still be preserved and after a time their original aesthetic value can be regained provided that new pointing is in a sympathetic colour and that the identities of the wall's components are not obscured by excessive mortar.

The guiding principle that should be followed when flint repairs to a wall are carried out is that the repaired work should as nearly as possible match the original. This may seem obvious, but it has often gone unheeded in the past. Fortunately, today's increasing awareness of the importance of sympathetic conservation gives reason to hope that not only the region's celebrated churches, but the houses, farms and boundary walls built with flints that are so essentially part of the East Anglian landscape, will from now on be sensitively maintained and so continue to delight the eye for many years to come.

Glossary

***

ARCADING A series of arches supported on columns or piers. *Blind* or *Blank Arcading*: arcading as a decorative theme applied to the surface of a wall, in relief or in flushwork.

AS-FOUND FLINT Pieces of flint as found in any of its natural forms, e.g. natural fragments, nodules, boulders, cobbles or pebbles etc.

ARRIS The edge or corner of a dressed stone or brick where two of its surfaces meet.

ASHLAR Squared freestone masonry wrought to even faces.

BAYS Subdivisions of a structure or elevation as defined by such features as columns, windows, etc. Also, projecting windows.

BED JOINT The horizontal mortar bedding between consecutive courses or layers of stone or brick in masonry walls.

BONDERS In flintwork, bricks, stones or larger pieces of flint, which are longer than the facing material, incorporated in a wall to assist in tying the facing into the body of the wall.

BOULDERS The rock constituents of boulder clay. Flint boulders are larger than cobbles but small enough to be held in one hand; they may be rounded, weathered or degraded.

CARSTONE A brown sandstone of the Cretaceous period used for building, which outcrops in west Norfolk between Hunstanton and Downham Market.

CHEQUER *See* Flintwork Patterns.

CINQUEFOIL *See* Trefoil.

COBBLES Rounded pieces of flint or other rock of any size between an orange and a coconut, of sundry oval or curvaceous shapes.

CORBELLING A continuous course or series of courses of stone or brick projecting from a wall, often supporting a structural element above.

CORE The inner body of a piece of flint beneath the cortex. It usually appears black when freshly fractured.

CORTEX The porous outer crust or rind on unworn flints. Initially white unless stained by ground pigments.

COURSE A continuous horizontal layer of bricks, stones or flints, etc. in a wall.

CRETACEOUS The geological period from 135 million years ago to 65 million years ago. *See* Geological Table.

CROCKETS Also *Crocketing*. In Gothic architecture, the knob-like carved features used to decorate the edges or angles of sloping elements, e.g. spires, canopies etc. *Crocketed*: decorated with crockets.

CROSS BOTONÉ A cross with limbs terminating in a trefoil.

CUSP The point between adjacent lobes of Gothic foliated tracery. It is part of the tracery framework.

DADO The lower part of a wall between the plinth and the window cill or the dado moulding.

DAGGER A two-foiled cusped Gothic tracery motif with unequal lobes. The smaller lobe may be rounded or pointed, and the larger is tapered and pointed.

DECORATED A stylistic division of Gothic architecture covering mainly the last decade of the thirteenth century and the first half of the fourteenth but lingering on into the second half. Characterized by ogee curves and curvilinear tracery.

DIAPER *See* Flintwork Patterns.

DRESSINGS Stonework or brickwork that forms the quoins of a building, or the jambs and heads of doorway and window openings etc.

DRIFT A geological term for superficial deposits laid down over the 'solid' formations of earlier eras.

EARLY ENGLISH A stylistic division of Gothic architecture covering the thirteenth century. Characterized by lancet windows and 'stiff leaf' foliage carving.

ERRATICS Boulders or fragments of rocks of any kind that have been displaced from their source by glacial action, found as the constituents of Drift.

FERRICRETE Dark brown concrete-like ferruginous conglomerate stone containing small pebbles or flint fragments in a finer-grained matrix. Also called *Puddingstone*.

FINIAL The topmost terminal feature of a pinnacle, spire, or gable, etc.

FLEMISH BOND The bonding arrangement of the facing bricks in a wall in which headers and stretchers alternate in all courses.

FLEMISH CHEQUER *See* Flintwork Patterns.

FLINTWORK PATTERNS Architectural reference works are sometimes ambiguous or inconsistent in the terminology used to describe the several different kinds of wall surface patterning, and so, in the absence of authoritative standard definitions, the expressions used in this book have the following meanings:

Check: a loose alternation of different materials.

Chequer, Chequerboard, Chequerwork: a pattern of squares, rectangles, or triangles of two materials, e.g. flint and stone, that are arranged in a chessboard pattern, essentially with the corners of the panels touching. Variations include *Diagonal Chequer*, where squares are set diagonally (sometimes called *Lozenge* or *Diamond* pattern), *Rectangular chequer*, where the panels of one or both materials are oblong, and *Triangular Chequer*, where the panels are three-sided.

Diaper (also called *Lattice, Trellis, Diamond*, or *Lozenge*): a repetitive pattern in two contrasting materials in which a criss-cross of diagonal 'lines' in one material forms a lattice pattern that defines sequences of diamonds or lozenges in the other material. Commonly, the pattern is made by brick headers in coursed flintwork, the bricks in successive courses being staggered relative to each other.

Flemish Chequer: a small-scale repetitive pattern in a coursed flint wall formed by brick headers that are set at about twice their own width apart with flints in between. This arrangement is repeated in every course with the brick headers being located centrally over the flints of the preceding course. The scale and character of this pattern is similar to Flemish Bond in ordinary brickwork.

Open Chequer: similar to Flemish Chequer but with the brick headers more widely spaced horizontally and vertically.

Panelling: in flushwork, the subdivision of a wall surface, by strips of freestone, into rectangular panels that are usually of vertical proportion, the stonework at the head of the panels often being foliated and cusped.

FLUSHWORK The use of freestone in combination with knapped flint to create flush patterns on a wall surface.

FOILS The lobes in Gothic tracery, i.e. those parts of the void enclosed by the tracery cusps.

FOLIATED Decorated with foils. Also, leaf carving.

FREESTONE Any even-grained type of stone that can be freely cut and worked in all directions.

GALLETING The decorative practice of inserting small pebbles or chips of flint, stone or brick into the exposed mortar joints of a wall.

GAULT BRICKS Buff-grey bricks made from gault clays obtained in parts of Cambridgeshire, Suffolk and west Norfolk.

HACKLY Descriptive of the condition of a flint or other piece of rock that has a rough, jagged broken surface.

HEADER In brickwork, the short end of a brick seen in the face of a wall.

HOODMOULD A projecting moulding in stone or brick above an arch or lintel whose purpose is to throw off water. When horizontal, also called a *Label*.

INDENTS In battlements, the lower zones of the parapet crenellations.

JAMBS The straight sides of a doorway or window opening.

JURASSIC The geological period from 195 million years ago to 135 million years ago. *See* Geological Table.

KNAPPED FLINT Flints which have been cut or split by man to present a flat surface of the core material, and also those which have been trimmed to regular shapes.

LABEL *See* Hoodmould.

LABEL STOP Projecting boss at the end of a hoodmould, normally at the arch springer point, and usually sculptured.

LACING COURSES Intermittent courses of a different material within a wall, e.g. brick courses in a flint wall, usually to assist in tying the facing into the body of the wall.

MERLONS In battlements, the raised zones of the parapet crenellations.

MOUCHETTE A curved variation of the Gothic dagger tracery motif.

MULTIFOIL *See* Trefoil.

NORMAN The post-Conquest Romanesque architectural style in Britain during the late eleventh and the twelfth centuries, characterized by round-headed arches.

OGEE A double curvature, comprising a concave and a convex curve. This shape is particularly associated with arches and tracery of the Decorated period.

OPEN CHEQUER *See* Flintwork Patterns

PANELLING *See* Flintwork Patterns

PATINATION A wax-like sheen on some corticated flint, attained by later assimilation of silica.

PEBBLES Small, rounded water-worn pieces of flint or other rock, about the size of a hen's egg, or smaller.

PERPENDICULAR A stylistic division of Gothic architecture covering the second half of the fourteenth century, the fifteenth and extending into the first half of the sixteenth century. Characterized by rectilinear tracery.

PERPENDS The vertical mortar joints between individual stones or bricks in masonry walls.

PLATBAND A flat horizontal band of stonework or brickwork that has a small projection from the general wall face.

PLIOCENE The geological period from 7 million years ago to 2 million years ago. *See* Geological Table.

PLINTH Projecting base course to a wall, buttress or pier, etc.

PUDDINGSTONE *See* Ferricrete.

PUTLOG HOLES Recesses, about 15 cm (6 in) square, left in the face of flint and stone walls during construction to accommodate horizontal members of the scaffolding.

QUATERNARY The geological period beginning about 2 million years ago during which Drift deposits were placed. *See* Geological Table

QUATREFOIL *See* Trefoil.

QUOINS The corner stones, bricks, or groups of bricks that form the external angles of a building.

RANGE Of a building, a distinct part or wing, often visually defined by the configuration of the roof.

RENDERING A cement or plaster coating to the surface of a wall.

REVEAL The return face of the masonry, splayed or at right-angles to the wall face, at the sides of door and window openings.

ROCK-FACING A type of carved textural rustication that is applied to stonework to create an impression of rugged, weathered natural rock.

RUSTICATION Accentuation of masonry or brickwork to give an enhanced effect of strength by means of projection, emphasized joints or extravagant surface textures.

SAXON The architectural style of the pre-Norman period in Britain.

SOLID FORMATIONS Geological term for pre-Quaternary formations laid down more than 2 million years ago and generally of a substantial thickness and a relatively regular extent.

SOUFFLET A quatrefoil which has one pair of opposite foils rounded and the other pair pointed.

SPANDREL The roughly triangular area of wall to the side of the curve of an arch, or between adjacent arches.

SPRINGING The level at which the curve of an arch rises from its supporting wall, pier, or column.

STAGE A subdivision of the height of a building, wall or feature into distinctive separate parts: usually defined by a horizontal architectural feature such as a string course, or a change in surface treatment.

STRETCHER In brickwork, the long side of a brick seen in the face of a wall.

STRING COURSE A projecting course or moulding of stone or brick running horizontally along the face of a wall.

TERTIARY The geological period from about 65 million years ago to about 2 million years ago. *See* Geological Table.

TRACERY Ornamental stone ribwork in the upper part of Gothic windows, in blank arches and screens and in flushwork. Also in church woodwork.

TREFOIL A motif of three lobes with cusps between them. The lobes may be rounded or pointed or a combination of both. It is extensively used as a decorative device in Gothic tracery, wall panelling and flushwork, etc.
Quatrefoil, Cinquefoil, Multifoil: as for Trefoil, but with four, five or many lobes, respectively.

UNDRESSED In stonework, natural, cleft or untooled stone.

VOUSSOIRS The wedge-shaped blocks forming an arch. The term is also used for bricks, stones or pieces of flint that are laid radially round an arch, though not wedge-shaped.

WHITE BRICKS An expression commonly used to describe the buff-grey bricks made from gault clay.

Geological Table

Era	Period	million years ago	Representative Materials
Cainozoic	Quaternary:		
	Recent		
	Pleistocene	.012–2	Erratics of older rocks, Ferricrete?
	Tertiary:		
	Pliocene	2–7	Coralline Crag
	Miocene	7–25	
	Oligocene	25–40	
	Eocene	40–55	Septaria
	Palaeocene	55–65	
Mesozoic	Cretaceous	65–135	Flints
			Chalk
			Hunstanton Red Rock
			Gault Clay: 'White' bricks
			Carstone
	Jurassic	135–195	Oxford Clay: Fletton bricks
			Oolitic Limestones
			e.g. Barnack, Clipsham, Ketton, Ancaster, Cotswold, Bath, Portland, etc.
			Collyweston Stone Slate
			Liassic Limestones
			e.g. Hornton, Ham Hill, etc.
	Triassic	195–225	New Red Sandstones
			e.g. Woolton, St Bees
Palaeozoic	Permian	225–280	Magnesian Limestones
			e.g. Mansfield, Roche Abbey
	Carboniferous	280–345	Carboniferous Limestones
			e.g. Yorkstone, Millstone Grit
			Coal
	Devonian	345–395	Delabole Slates
	Silurian	395–440	Cumbrian Blue/Black Slate
	Ordovician	440–500	Lake District Green Slate
			Welsh Slate
	Cambrian	500–600	Welsh Slate
Pre-Cambrian		600–	Basalt, Granites

Bibliography

Baggallay, F. T., 'The Use of Flint in Buildings especially in the County of Suffolk', *R.I.B.A. Transactions*, New Series, Vol.1, pp.105–24, 1885

Brunskill, R. W., *Illustrated Handbook of Vernacular Architecture*, Faber, 3rd edn, 1987

Chatwin, C. P., *British Regional Geology: East Anglia and Adjoining Areas*, H.M.S.O. 1961

Clifton Taylor, A., *The Pattern of English Building*, Faber, 4th edn, 1987

Clifton Taylor, A., and Ireson, A. S., *English Stone Building*, Gollancz 1983

Mason, H. J., *Flint, the Versatile Stone*, Providence Press 1978

Parsons, D., and others, *Stone, Quarrying and Building in England, AD 43–1525*, Phillimore 1990

Pevsner, N. and others, *The Buildings of England*, Penguin: *Cambridgeshire* 1970, *Essex* 1965, *North East Norfolk and Norwich* 1962, *North West and South Norfolk* 1962, *Suffolk* 1974

Shepherd, W., *Flint: Its Origin, Properties and Uses*, Faber 1972

Wright, A., *Craft Techniques for Traditional Buildings*, Batsford 1991

Index of Place Names

The illustrations are indexed by their numbers, in brackets: black and white ones are in roman figures and the colour ones are in italic.
B = Bedfordshire, C = Cambridgeshire, E = Essex, N = Norfolk, S = Suffolk

General Index